Acknowledg

Special thanks to all the people that contributed to this book by contacting me through my blog, your questions and comments made the writing of this book possible. Demy, Johnny, Graham Anderson, Marco, Duke Nukem, and Bleepbloop just to name a few! And to all the people I know who have promoted my blog through Reddit and social media - UnsungSaviour16, Uberg33k, and MinnesotaNice- You guys are awesome! Thanks to the friendly folks at Gambrinus Malting. I am especially grateful to my wife and children for not only putting up with all of my experiments in our tiny kitchen but actually encouraging me to do so.

Table of Contents

Table of Contents	2
Introduction	4
Malting Simplified	7
Getting started	10
Equipment and some Terminology	10
Steeping, Germination, Kilning and Curing	16
Moisture Content	21
Growing and Harvesting	24
Threshing and Winnowing	33
Feed Barley	35
Recipes: Pale Malt	39
Pilsner/ Lager Malt	43
Historical Malting	47
Modern Malting	53
Vienna Malt	56
Toasted Malts	58
Victory, Biscuit and Amber	58
The Melanoidin Family	61
Aromatic, Munich, and Melanoidin Malts	61
Brumalt	61
Munich Malt	63
Melanoidin/ Brumalt	72

Caramel Malts 74

Special B Type Malt 76

Making Caramel malt from Pale malt 77

Roasted Malts 78

Chocolate, Roasted Malt, Roasted Barley 78

Debittered Black Patent Malt 80

Brown Malts 82

Acid Malt 89

Wheat 90

Oats 91

Spelt and Emmer 92

Bibliography 93

Introduction

As homebrewers we all know the joys of creating our own beer. I'm sure we can all remember tasting our first homebrew, good or bad, and equally remember tasting our first all-grain brew. Now imagine the satisfaction of tasting a beer that was made entirely from barley that you grew and malted yourself. If you've already used your own homegrown hops in your beer you'll know the feeling. When I first started malting my own barley I honestly would have been happy with a mediocre beer. I wasn't expecting much, so I was shocked (and extremely happy) when my beer actually improved using my own malts. There's a freshness and depth of flavour to them that I haven't experienced with store bought malts. I've also seen great improvements with the head retention in my beers. Expect to see some big rocky billowing clouds of foam that just won't leave your glass. Some of my beers have even won medals in local homebrewing contests and I can safely say that the beers that did not place did so because of some brewing error and not because of the malt. When you malt your own barley you have the opportunity to invent your own special malts and they will be completely unique, no other malt will taste like the malt you make. There are so many variables in the production of malt that this uniqueness is inevitable and if that alone isn't reason enough to try, it's just plain fun. It's a hobby in itself and sometimes I get so wrapped up in making malt that I forget to brew. Needless to say I often amass quite a collection of homemade malts that usually end up as gifts.

There is an obvious downside to malting at home. Certainly, it's not worth doing simply to save money. Store bought malt is cheap, especially considering what's involved in producing it. And given the amount of time, energy and extra gizmos and gadgets you may accumulate this isn't a money saving endeavour. Even though some of us may have gotten into homebrewing to save money I think most brewers end up with a passion to make good beer and it's the same with malting. Our goal is to produce a great quality beer that you can be proud to share with your friends. So be warned, malting is a hobby that is as involved as brewing itself. How far you take this hobby is up to you. You may want to stick to small batches of specialty malts to add your own signature to your beers or you may want to "brew the hard way" and make all the malts for your beer. Personally I do a little of both, some batches are 100% homemade, others have store bought base malts. Malting takes a lot of time and patience, about 10 days from start to finish. Your oven may be occupied for days at a time. You may find yourself getting up several times in the middle of the night to monitor your temperatures or to change your steep water, it's a hobby that can become an obsession, but as homebrewers this is nothing new, right?

A downside to growing barley is that it involves some risk and requires some space. Your crop may fail for various reasons like hungry birds, rats or even thieves. You can expect to grow about 10 lbs per 100 sq. feet. This can vary from 5-15 lbs. I have managed to grow 20 lb per 100 sq.ft. one year by planting intensively. One of the reasons I started growing my own barley was because my local homebrew shop didn't carry Marris Otter and I kept reading recipes calling for it so I decided to take matters into my own hands and grow my own. Little did I know that securing some Marris Otter seed was nearly impossible, but that's another story. These days where I live there is a craft beer boom happening and there are plenty of malts to choose from at the homebrew supply shops including Marris Otter. So why bother growing barley you may ask?

Malting is fun, growing barley is even more fun. To me it's like magic and connects me to my beers like a vintner is connected to their wine. When I throw barley seeds into my garden in early spring I always think how impossible it seems that anything will grow and yet it does. I'm also fascinated by the whole malting process. You're tricking seeds into sprouting. The seed embryo comes to life and produces enzymes that partially hydrolyze the food reserves in the endosperm, making them more soluble. Mashing will continue the process by utilizing the enzymes to convert all the remaining starch into sugar. It's one part gardening, one part cooking and one part playing god. You're taking part in a process that's been practiced by humankind for thousands of years and you get to be the director, guiding things along, steering it one way or another, encouraging it's progression and creating something amazing out of virtually nothing.

This book includes recipes that I have accumulated over the past 6 years through research and experimentation. They should be viewed as mere guidelines or suggestions because everyone's conditions will vary. The type of barley, it's protein content, the humidity, your malt kiln, your water and so on will all affect your malt. This is a biological process so your barley will have its own personality. I have tested each recipe in this book but there are many variables in malting so if a recipe doesn't work for you, don't give up, hopefully I've included enough information that you can troubleshoot and find the variable that needs tweaking. However, the science of malting is complex and vast and I have greatly oversimplified several aspects of it in order to keep things brief. The main purpose of writing this book was to compile all the malting recipes that I have collected into one place that's easier to access than the octopus that my blog has become. I hope you find it informative and useful. Cheers, and happy malting!

Malting Simplified

Here's the process in a nutshell. What we're doing is tricking our barley into growing just a little but not too much. We start by steeping the barley in water until it absorbs a specific amount of water. That amount will help determine how much the barley grows. During germination the barley starts to develop the all important enzymes we will need in brewing. Certain malts require more modification and therefore more moisture like Munich malt. Others require less and will be less modified like Pilsner malt.

The longer we can germinate, without overgrowing the grain, the more enzymes we develop. Certain barley varieties have the ability to develop more enzymes than others like most 6-row barleys. However, if we're not careful the barley can overgrow. The sprout grows longer than the length of the kernel and will turn green. The food reserves are then utilized by the new plant leaving nothing for us brewers. When this happens the malt will taste bitter and grassy, like the sprout it has become. So we want to slow the growth and draw out the germination stage for as long as possible and we can do this by lowering the temperature or drying out the malt just a little. This is called withering. Sometimes the opposite can happen and the barley does not grow enough. In this case you may have to spray a little water on the malt on the third or fourth day to encourage some more growth.

The malt is considered modified when the endosperm cell walls have broken down and the starches are now available to be acted upon by the enzymes. You can tell that the starch cell walls have broken down when you can rub the starch between your fingers to a smooth chalky paste. If not the starch will be gummy and form small balls. Once the malt is considered modified it's ready to be kilned and we now have a bank of enzymes to utilize in order to make different types of malt.

Enzymes need moisture to work and are activated at specific temperatures during kilning and to a greater extent during stewing (kilning with no ventilation). Just like in brewing temperatures in the 32-43°C 90-110°F range will activate beta glucanase, enzymes which help break down the beta glucans likewise, temperatures in the 45-55°C 113-131°F will activate the proteolytic enzymes which will act on the available proteins in the malt. Breaking down the proteins will lead to melanoidin production which is responsible for the rich malty flavours and colour compounds that are in Munich malt, Aromatic, and Melanoidin malt. If we utilize the Saccharification temperatures, 65-70°C 149-158°F while the malt is wet then we get caramel malts. Length of time, the amount of moisture present and the amount of enzymes available will affect the level of Saccharification.

For base malts we want to keep as much diastatic power as possible. Drying the malt below 45°C 113°F will ensure that most of the enzymes used in mashing are not activated and remain intact. Enzymes like beta glucanase will be and has the effect of degrading the beta glucans in the malt which is important for reducing viscosity in the beer and increasing the malts friability. Once the enzymes have been utilized they are spent and our diastatic power has been reduced. However, when the malt is dry (under 10%) enzymes are no longer at risk of being activated even at higher temperatures. This enzyme dormancy is how we can cure malt, drying it further (for better storage) and adding flavour and colour without severely damaging or activating the enzymes. But enzymes are not invincible and some of them will be destroyed during kilning lowering our diastatic power. Severe damage occurs if the curing temperature goes above 105°C 221°F even when dry.

This is why dark roasted malts will have zero diastatic power. However, lightly toasted malts will maintain some diastatic power. The roasted or even the lightly toasted malts can be made with any base malt either pale or lager since the temperatures for these surpass pale malt kilning temperatures. You can make these from a store bought base malt in a standard oven without any special equipment. Amber, Victory, Biscuit as well as Chocolate and Black Patent malt can all start from a base malt.

Kilning is carried out with a lot of airflow and low temperatures at first as the surface moisture evaporates easily. As time goes on the temperature is increased and not as much airflow is necessary. Once the moisture is below 10% as previously explained we can now cure the malt which is necessary to drive off the remaining moisture within the grain and to add flavour and

colour. Curing is also important for a malts friability or it's ability to be crushed. Without curing, the malt will be hard and steely and as you know a bad crush will affect our final gravity.

The final step is to remove the roots which is done at home by rubbing the malt over a sieve. If the malt is well cured these should be brittle and fall off easily. If not cured enough, these rootlets will be flexible and nearly impossible to remove. The rootlets are also hygroscopic meaning they will re-absorb moisture through the air to become flexible again so it is important to remove them soon after kilning.

Getting started
Equipment and some Terminology

Here's what you need:

Barley. If you're lucky and live near a farmer that grows barley you have the best source available. If you grow it yourself you can expect anywhere from 5-15 lbs per 100 sq. feet. Otherwise there are a few options for barley. Some health food stores sell hulled and/or hulless barley. Hulled barley has had its husk removed mechanically. Hulless barley refers to certain varieties of barley that have a loose husk that falls off when harvested. They will still sprout, but like wheat, you will need 10% by weight in rice hulls to brew with them or you will have a stuck sparge. And then there's feed barley, available at farm animal feed stores. Inexpensive yes, but you get what you pay for. I've made some pretty good beers with feed barley so I've included a chapter on it. Since it's so cheap it's good barley to experiment with.

Most malting companies clean and grade the barley themselves. By grading I mean they sift out all the small grains leaving only the plump ones which are over 2.2 - 2.4mm. depending on the variety of barley being used. This makes for a more consistent germination. They will also have tested the protein content and tested for fungus or mould to make sure it's ideal for malting. Selling graded malting quality barley would be a valuable service to the home maltster. Unfortunately, none of them do this yet.

Steeping Containers: Basically any container will do as long as it can hold water and is clean. I use small plastic trays that I got at a dollar store to do small batches because they hold two pounds of grain with room for steep water and they're easy to handle.They also fit very nicely in my fermenting fridge. For bigger batches I've used plastic buckets and rubbermaid bins.

Nylon mesh sample bag: If steeping a large amount of grain you can use a small nylon mesh sample bag with a pre-measured amount of barley to use for weighing and determining your moisture contents throughout the process until the curing stage. I've found some that weigh next to nothing so I can just take it out of the steep tank or kiln and throw it on the scale to monitor the progress. I've also seen some people use a small container or box made with perforated metal or screening with the advantage that you can use this during curing.

Green malt: This is malt that has germinated but has not been kilned yet.

Water: Use filtered water or unchlorinated water. Chlorine has the same effect in malting as it does in brewing and will contribute phenolic flavours so avoid it as much as possible. When doing a large batch ½ campden tablet (crushed) per 10 gallons of water will take care of the chlorine. You'll have plenty of time to treat your water between steeping during the air rests.

Temperature: This is key, you must either have the ability to control the temperature or you do your malting during the spring and fall when the outside temperatures are ideally around 10-15°C 50-60°F. In my area this usually lasts a couple of months from October to December and then again in February and March. This is when I'll do large batches of malt. I do small batches throughout the year in my brewing fridge which I have hooked up to a temperature controller.

Thermometers: Along with the ones you already have for brewing with I'd recommend a probe thermometer, the kind with a cable so you can keep the probe in the grain bed and easily read the temperature of the grain without opening the kiln.

A Kiln: Any container where you have the ability to control the heat and airflow/ ventilation. This is not as easy as it sounds because you need low temperatures, too low for most ovens. Large dehydrators work well for the kilning stage but may not be hot enough for curing so you still have to use your oven for this last stage.

My first malting experiments were in my oven but instead of turning the oven on I put a hot-plate inside to act as a heat source. I made screens for the malt out of some plywood and metal window screening. This worked extremely well, but nobody else in the family shared my excitement when the oven was occupied for days at a time. The hot-plates that come with a temperature dial are great because you can control the temperature and maintain the low temperatures you'll need. I have marks made on my hotplate dial indicating 35°C with fan "on" and 45°C with fan "off". I also have marks for 50°C (for Munich or Brumalt) and 70°C or 158°F for Caramel malt. For anything higher I will use my oven. It's lowest temperature is 170°F. For another heat source you can use incandescent light bulbs connected to a dimmer switch to control the temperature, the problem is you'll have to change the bulbs and these are getting harder to find these days.

The first oven that I used had a vent hole in one of the stove elements so I put a small fan over the hole to pull the air through. Most ovens also have some vent space at the bottom of the door where the air can enter the oven. This is also a useful space to run the power cord through. The oven I have now has a smaller vent hole that comes out under the control panel. A small computer fan could be attached on the inside of the oven's vent hole but I didn't think it was necessary since I was only doing small batches under 5 pounds. Anything over 5 lbs and I would recommend a fan of some sort. To cure the malt at higher temperatures be sure to remove the hotplate and fan before turning the oven on, this seems obvious but speaking from experience it's easy to forget.

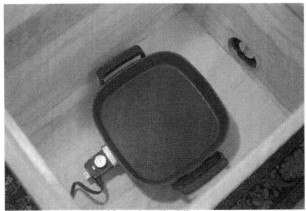

Hot plate in kiln

Building your own kiln: The kiln I use now which you can see on my blog and Youtube channel is simply a plywood box with a fan hole at the bottom. There are vent holes on the top that I can close off and there is a perforated metal tray inside to hold the malt. The heat source is the same hotplate I used in my oven. It's a real bonus to have a dedicated space for malting so that you're not taking up the oven for days at a time. My current kiln can dry up to 40 pounds (dry weight) at one time. It's made of ¾ inch plywood so the wood does provide some insulation. It was intended for 50 lbs but I didn't take into account that germinated barley takes up about twice the space as raw dry barley. I still have to use my oven for the curing stage so I made the tray removable and the same size as my oven so that I can transfer it easily. A more deluxe version would have a variable speed fan to have more control over the air-flow, and perhaps an insulated metal lid to avoid the warping that occurs with plywood. Also having the ability to control both heat and airflow with a programmable micro-controller would be a real luxury. You can see an example of this on my blog, just look for Dimitris' set-up using an arduino micro-controller.

My homemade kiln.

Industrial kilns actually use very powerful fans which are necessary to blow the warm air through 4 feet of barley. Ideally if you're using something like a 25 watt fan the malt bed shouldn't be more than 6" deep to dry the malt effectively. When planning your kiln design consider that 10 lbs dry barley when germinated will take up about 1 square foot at 5.5 - 6" deep but this does depend on root growth and how wilted your malt has become. It will also be heavier due to the water content, 10 lbs will weigh around 14 lbs when germinated. My malt kiln tray is 18"x24" which is 3 square feet. So 30 lb.(dry weight) which is a manageable amount will make a 5.5" bed. Historically most malt houses kilned with no more than a 4" deep bed of malt, but that was before fans were employed and kilns relied on the natural draft of the malt house. I've malted 40 lbs. at one time in my kiln with a bed that started at 7.5" but I think this is the upper limit for my 25 watt fan. Drying was quite slow.

Perforated steel tray inside.

Curing: For curing I recommend using your oven, you don't need ventilation at this point and an oven is much safer to use at curing temperatures. I did manage to cure that 40 lbs. of malt in my oven, but again I think 30 lbs is more manageable maximum amount for a standard size oven.

Rootlets or culms: The last stage in the malting process is to get rid of the rootlets. They're high in protein and may contribute a bitter flavour. If your malt is dry enough they should fall off when the barley is rubbed over a sieve. If they are not falling off easily you may want to cure your malt for another couple of hours. Buy the largest, sturdiest sieve you can find to save yourself some time.

Steeping, Germination, Kilning and Curing

Steeping: The first step in malting is tricking our barley grains into growing for us. Yet we only want them to grow to a certain point. If they grow too much we get bitter tasting sprouts, too little and our malt is considered undermodified and may not fully convert when mashed. Ideally we want all of our barley grains to grow to that certain point at the same time, which is a lot to ask of a bunch of seeds. The key to ensure that all of this happens is moisture content. Maltsters have figured out exact percentages of moisture content to ensure even germination that will reach the desired state of modification. For Pale malts it's 42-44 % for pilsner it's a little less from 38-41% and for Munich and Brumalt it's quite high 44-48% In the next chapter I'll explain how we can find the moisture content of barley and how to calculate our target steep weight.

In modern malting steeps are interrupted with air rests so that the barley can absorb oxygen. This speeds up the germination process dramatically. There have been many experiments made in the past with different steep schedules and steep temperatures. Their main objective was to reduce germination time while maintaining uniform growth. Some had long (24 hour) air rests and some had very short steeps. The steep schedule I use consists of 8 hour steeps followed by 8 hour air rests where the water is simply drained off. I find keeping the 8 hour schedule is easy to manage. If you start at 6 am then you can drain the barley at 2 pm and then soak it again at 10 pm. and then continue the next morning at 6 am. I also think it's a good idea to keep track of the number of steeps you do because it's easy to forget over a couple of days. Air rests are important and I'd say it's better to have an air rest that goes over 8 hours than under and as for steeps it's better to have a shorter steep than 8 hours than a longer one. Historically (before the 20th century) maltsters would submerge their barley for long periods without air rests which, along with using cooler temperatures, has the effect of delaying germination and slowing the growth. Air rests are a relatively new development (within the last 150 years) and has significantly sped up the whole process of malting, germination starts earlier and growth is more rapid.

I've read quite a few instructions on steeping barley using an aquarium aeration stone submerged in the steep water and not including an air rest. When I've tried this I ended up with a very uneven germination. Some kernels grew very fast and overshot and other hardly grew at all. These grains were probably not getting a consistent amount of oxygen so I wouldn't recommend this method.

Water is also as important to your steeping as it is to your brewing. Use filtered water to avoid chlorine. It has the same effect on your malt as it does in your beer and will contribute phenolic flavours so it's something to avoid. Mineral content can affect the rate at which the grain absorbs water not that it really matters just something to know. Water with a high mineral content will be absorbed slower than water with a low mineral content.

Using a fan that blows air down through the grain during the air rest can also speed things up as this has the effect of removing any carbon dioxide produced by the barley and it also dries the surface moisture from the grain. Once the surface of the grain is dry it will absorb more oxygen.

Temperature: Keep it at 10-12°C or 50-54°F for steeping. Keeping it cold slows the rate at which the barley absorbs water but keeps bacteria from forming. During my first attempt at malting I steeped at room temperature. After the second steep things smelled kind of sour, like yogurt. After the third steep things got nasty. The bacteria had multiplied rapidly and when I kilned it our whole apartment smelled like a pig farm and the smell lasted for days.

Germination: This is where the magic happens. The grain starts to grow and as it does it will start to produce enzymes. It's our job to encourage the development of as many enzymes as possible so the malt has a high diastatic power and will convert all those starches during mashing.

You may notice even during the last steep that a small white bump has appeared on the end of the grain. If it's already there during the last steep, keep an eye on the water content as the grain will absorb water faster once the "chitting" has started. These small bumps will become the roots within a couple of days. They grow fast and may even start to tangle together. This is one of the reasons for turning the malt.

Another reason for turning the malt is to cool it down, the respiration process can create a lot of heat and we want to keep the grain around 12-15°C. Keeping it cool also discourages mould growth. Another byproduct of respiration is carbon dioxide which if allowed to accumulate can stop the growth of the grain. By turning the malt you're re-introducing oxygen into the bed.

Turning the grain depends on the temperature but turn at least every 8 hours or so. Turn more often when the malt heats up. I think this is the most enjoyable part of malting, this is where you feel like Dr. Frankenstein and exclaim "It's alive!"

After a couple of days you should be able to see the acrospires. This is the plant shoot which you will see on the smooth side of the kernel underneath the hull. Sometimes you have to break the hull apart to see it. Once they grow on average to ¾ of the total length of the grain then the malt should be modified. However, this is not the best indicator just the easiest visual one.

A better indicator of modification is the "rub" test. To do this break apart the hull and push out as much of the starchy contents of the grain as you can onto your finger. Rub the starchy material against your finger with your thumb. If the starches gum up into small balls and roll across your finger the malt is not fully modified. If the starch smears across your finger as a smooth paste then you're modified

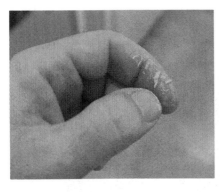
Not yet modified

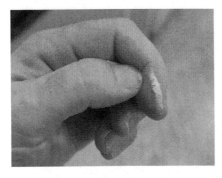
Modified.

Historically after germination the malt was piled up and allowed to "mellow" for a day. This may have allowed enough carbon dioxide to build up to stop the growth. Another practice was to "wilt" the malt after germinating by spreading the bed out thin enough to air dry. In both methods growth may stop but enzyme development would continue. These steps are no longer used in modern malting. To wilt your malt at home simply spread the malt out on a screen to dry out a little. You'll see that once the roots shrink the acrospire will stop growing. I recommend doing this as it is a way of extending your germination time. The longer the malt takes the better. With air rests germination usually takes 5-6 days.

Kilning: This refers to the drying of the malt. For base malts drying takes place below 50°C 122°F until the moisture content of the malt is below 10%. Above 50°C and the enzymes are activated. When the malt is dry enough the enzymes can withstand higher temperatures up to 105°C or 221°F Above this temperature, the enzymes are destroyed.

Most kilning schedules utilize fans that push air through the grain bed. The moisture on the outer layers of the malt will evaporate during this first phase. At a certain point however fans are slowed down and the temperature will be raised to drive the moisture out of the inside of the kernel. Every malting company has their own kilning schedules which can depend on many factors such as type of barley, weather/humidity, volume of malt, and volume or rate at which the air passes through the grain.

Curing: This is where a lot of the flavour and colour changes occur and where the temperatures are raised to bring the moisture content down to below 5%. It is only when the malt moisture is below 5% that the enzymes are rendered inactive. This makes the malt stable for storage. Temperatures range from 170°F for pilsner to 190°F for pale and even higher for Vienna and Munich malts.

Friability: Once dry your malt becomes friable. Friability refers to how easily the malt can be crushed. An indicator of friability is the condition of the roots. If they come off easily when rubbed on a sieve then your grain is dry and friable if they are still hanging on and refuse to break off, then pop your malt back into your oven for a couple more hours. Friability is also dependant on the level of modification, the more modified it is, the easier it will be to crush. Another factor which can affect friability is kilning. If your malt temperature reaches 60°C 140°F while there is still over 10% moisture the starch is said to gelatinize (De Clerck vol.1 p.182) which leads to very hard, steely malt, (sort of like dried pasta).

Moisture Content

Stop right there! Do not even think about skipping this chapter! This is required reading. Knowing the moisture content of your malt throughout the whole malting process is key to making good malt. So consider yourself warned, you may be able to make malt without knowing but your efficiency will suffer and your conversion may take hours. It's also good to know so that you can repeat your process and be consistent.

The first step in the malting process is steeping but we have to know how long to steep for. Pilsner malts are not steeped as long as Pale for example. Our goal is to achieve a specific moisture content within the barley. The moisture content will determine the level of modification your barely will reach and can range from 38%-48%. Pilsner malt is usually steeped to a moisture content of 38-42% and is most often considered undermodified. Pale malt is 42-46%. Munich on the other hand is often steeped till reaching 46-48% moisture content and is highly modified. Without moisture the barley will stop growing so limiting the amount of water the grain can utilize is a way of controlling the level of growth.

During kilning the relationship between temperature and moisture content have an effect on colour, flavour and the diastatic power of the malt. For example kilning above 50°C 122°F when there is over 10% moisture content will activate enzymes in the malt lowering your diastatic power but doing this can enhance the malty flavours in your malt. For example Munich malt is kilned at 60°C 140°F when it's moisture content is at 25-30% but more about that later. The best kilning schedules show you the moisture contents and the temperature. Unfortunately this information is often unavailable as malting companies are very protective of their recipes.

Step 1. Determining the initial moisture content: Barley after harvesting usually has about a 10-12% moisture content but this varies depending on humidity and the weather at harvest etc. Malting barley should be stored at no higher than a 13.5% moisture content. So the first step is to find out exactly what the current moisture content of your barley is. To do this take a one ounce sample of crushed barley weighed with a microscale so you can be as accurate as possible. It's important that it is crushed so that it dries out completely. Put it in an oven proof dish or pan in your oven at 225°F for 3 hours, this will dry out your barley completely so it's "bone dry"

Once you weigh it again the difference in weight X 100 will be the current moisture percentage of your barley. For example if in your one ounce sample your "bone dry" weight is now .9 of an ounce, the difference in weight is .1 of an ounce x 100 = 10% moisture content.

Step 2. Target Steep Weight:

So now we know the current moisture content and the 'bone dry" weight of the barley. When you start steeping we need to know how much our barley will weigh at a certain moisture percentage. That way we just have to weigh it to find out what percentage the moisture content is at. This is our target steep weight. This is the total weight of the barleys dry matter plus it's water content. To figure this out **take the bone dry weight of the barley being malted and divide it by the dry matter percentage you're aiming for.**

For example let's say you're making 10 lbs of pale malt and the moisture content you're aiming for is 42% This means the dry matter content of the barley makes up 58% of the target steep weight.

Let's pretend you've figured out that your barley is starting at 10% moisture which means the bone dry weight of the 10lbs is 9lbs.

Divide the 9 lbs by .58 (58 divided by 100 because we're dealing with percentage) = 15.5 lbs. This is our target steep weight.
To check: 15.5 x .42 (%) = 6.5 lbs. water
            15.5 - 6.5 = 9 lbs bone dry barley (dry matter)

Clear as mud?
I like to record the moisture content of my barley, that way I can refer to it for every batch. As long as I'm malting the batches within a month or two. Any longer and you might want to measure the moisture content again.

Let's try the same amount but with a 38% target moisture content as if we were making a pilsner malt.
9 lb divided by .62 (since 100-38 = 62) = 14.5 lbs. Our target steep weight
To check 14.5 x .38 (%) = 5.5 lbs water
            14.5 - 5.5 = 9 lbs bone dry barley.

Growing and Harvesting

Lucky for us barley grows in a wide variety of climates and growing it is not as hard as it may sound. Barley doesn't need much, in fact it does better in light soils which are low in nitrogen. A soil pH of 6.5 is recommended. Irrigation may be necessary depending on your climate and soil but should be avoided later in the growing season to reduce the chance of mold and fungus.

Space: Yields vary depending on a number of factors but as a rough guide 800 square feet can give you about 50 lbs. of barley. So a garden that's 20 ft. by 40 ft. could potentially give enough barley to brew five times in a year or a year's supply of specialty grains.

Seeding rates also vary, but studies have shown that the ideal plant density is considered to be 20-25 plants per square foot. If plants are too crowded there's a risk of fungus developing and seed heads can be small. On the other hand plant too sparsely and weeds can flourish. Also with more space plants may send out more tillers producing heads that may not be ripe at harvest.

Depending on the germination rate of your seed and the number of critters around it's always good to plant some extra, I usually shoot for 30-35 seeds per square foot. Seed can be broadcast and raked in but planting in rows ensures a more even depth. Having rows also makes it easier to weed. Row spacing is usually 6-8 inches apart. Row widths can be up to 5 inches wide. Seeds should be 1-2.5 inches deep. Remay or some sort of row cover fabric can help deter birds for the first two weeks while the plants are emerging.

There are two types of barley 2-rowed and 6-row which refers to how many rows of kernels are on the seed head. Most malting barleys are two rowed as these have more consistently sized kernels and have slightly thinner husks. However, 6-rowed varieties tend to have higher enzyme contents which make them suitable for brewing with adjuncts.

Barley varieties are also divided into either Winter or Spring types as some barleys yield more when planted in the fall to be ready early in the summer and other barleys do better when planted in the early spring, to be harvested in the late summer. There is a higher yield potential with Winter barley but this comes with the risk of seedling frost damage and a greater chance for disease development and pest damage. Traditionally 6-rowed barleys were winter barleys and 2-row were planted in the spring but with newer varieties this is no longer the rule.

Lodging: This has been my biggest challenge next to hungry critters. Lodging refers to when the grain falls over due to too much nitrogen in the soil. This usually happens after the heads start forming, if the stalks are too weak they won't be able to hold the weight of the heads and the plant falls over. This will happen in clumps after a rain or if there is some wind to knock them around. Too much nitrogen also increases the amount of protein in your grain but having too little will decrease your overall yield. It's virtually impossible to get the grain upright again after this happens, sometimes it may straighten on it's own only to fall again later. Once the barley has lodged it's subject to mould due to the lack of air-flow and all the critters that can and will inhabit your garden like mice, rats, and birds. Because the grain is close to the ground they will find it and throw a party and invite all their friends, all thanks to your hard work. Also depending on the severity of the bending the grain may not develop properly afterwards and the kernels will be small. Barley farmers sometimes use growth inhibitors to prevent lodging from happening. For the home grower there are some things you can do. There are test kits available at garden stores to measure the nitrogen, phosphorus and potassium levels in your soil. Avoid manure applications, instead try an organic fertilizer which contains a lot of other nutrients and is low in nitrogen. A well made compost will contain a balance of nutrients that are good for your garden. Seaweed makes fantastic compost, if you have access to it.

My last resort for lodging: As a garden scale grain grower losing some of your crop means less beer for you, never mind all the work you put in prepping the soil, seeding weeding, and watering. After losing an entire crop one year to rats and birds after my grain lodged I was determined to prevent this from happening again. I came up with a method for supporting the grain stalks using chicken wire. This method requires a bit of an investment but works well. Basically I use chicken wire that's 4 feet wide over the length of the garden. It's laid flat but suspended about two feet off the ground with stakes. Thin bamboo poles 4 ft. long tied to the stakes can support the chicken wire about every 5 ft. The barley grows through the chicken wire and adds just enough support to keep it upright. So for a garden that's 20 ft. by 40 ft. you would need 8- 20 ft. rows that are 4 ft. wide and have 1 foot in between them. That's 160 ft. of chicken wire, 40 4 ft. pieces of bamboo and 80 4 ft. stakes which you can re-use. I used this method to grow 39 lbs. of barley on 200 sq. feet. one year. To do this I planted very intensively, about 45 seeds per square foot and I didn't hold back on the manure either. I just wanted to see what would happen. The plants that grew would have fallen over for sure had it not been for the chicken wire and I was lucky that year that no mould developed as the plants were very overcrowded. I have not had this grain tested for protein levels but it's probably

pretty high. It still made great beer though!

Critters: Animals love barley, when they discover it in your garden they'll stop at nothing to get as much as they can. I've watched rats and birds chew the bottoms of the stalks and then pull the plants down to get the seed head, it's pretty comical. To avoid them you have to make sure they don't discover the barley in you garden. This is why it's important to keep all the seed heads from getting close to the ground. Having a fast ripening barley also helps. This means good weather and good timing are important. Also, most newer varieties of barley ripen faster than older varieties . Speaking of timing, the time that you plant will obviously affect the time it's ready to harvest. The advantage of fall planting is that you get a jump on the weeds. You also have more time for the crop to dry out when the weather is good. I tried planting in the fall one year so that the barley would be ready in the early summer. The barley was ready before anything else in my garden and the surrounding gardens so food sources for animals at this time were sparse. This was the year the critters got everything. I think the birds were especially hungry at that time of year and found a great source of carbs in my garden. The following year I planted in the early spring so that the barley would be ready in the late summer and they only discovered it a day or two before I harvested it so they hardly got any. One year when I grew Harrington (a two-row) and Robust (which is a 6 row barley) they left the Robust alone but went after the 2 row variety even though some of the Robust had fallen over. My theory on this is that on a six row head of barley the rows surround the head and are protected by the prickly hairs on each seed, whereas on a two row head the hairs are in two neat rows on either side of the head. Perhaps it was easier to access the seeds on these heads as opposed to working around the sharp hairs of the six row. Larger critters like raccoons and squirrels can do a lot of damage. One deterrent that I've found works well, at least for a short time is cayenne pepper. Sprinkle this all over your garden even on your barley heads, as long as you're a week away from harvesting. I've found that this seems to work better for raccoons than squirrels.

Insects: Barley Thrips, Cereal Leaf Beetle, Grasshoppers, Wheat Stem Sawfly, and Wireworms are a few of the insects that can damage your crop.

Common Viral diseases:

Barley Stripe Mosaic Virus: Yellow streaks or spots. Spread through infected seed, can stunt growth.

Barley Yellow Dwarf Virus: A virus that affects most cereal crops. It is spread by aphids and symptoms include yellowing of leaves, reduced root growth, delayed or no heading, reduction in yield, as well heads can become black during ripening due to colonization of saprotrophic fungi.
Insecticide or other means of controlling aphid populations should be used as soon as possible. Yellowing leaves can be mistaken for a nitrogen deficiency.

Oat Blue Dwarf Virus: Transferred by Leafhoppers. Symptoms include severe stunting, shortened and stiffened leaves, a proliferation of lateral tillers and sometimes a bluish green colour.

Powdery Mildew: Appears as fluffy grey patches on the upper surfaces of leaves. Prevalent in cool wet climates or where plants are overcrowded.

Spot Blotch Symptoms: Small dark brown spots first appearing on the leaf. Over time the lesions become darker and more circular to elongated

Net Blotch Symptoms: A light to dark brown spot will initially appear on the leaf surface. As the lesion matures, a net-like pattern will form within lesions. Eventually, lesions will combine and can cause severe defoliation

Scald or Barley Leaf Blotch Symptoms: Leaf spots tend to be oval with a water-soaked appearance. Lesions eventually have a tan to bleach white center surrounded by a dark brown margin.

Foot Rot (root rot): Soil borne disease symptoms include dark lesions near the base of the leaves. May result in stunted growth or plant death.

Smut: "There are two types of smut: covered smut and loose smut. Covered smut is externally seed-borne, spread by spores from diseased plant heads to the surface of healthy seeds. The disease is favoured by seeding into cold soil in late fall and early spring. Covered smut can stunt plants, blacken kernels and deform awns.

Loose smut: is internally seed-borne, and barley has poor resistance to the disease. Spores from smutted heads are dispersed by wind or rain to healthy heads, where they infect the developing grain. The disease thrives in cool, wet, July weather.

Infected seed will appear normal and will germinate. However, the following year, after germination, the fungus will grow with the plant and replace the head with spores. Plants will appear normal until heading, when infected heads will be visibly black and filled with dusty spores." (Alberta Barley Organization)

Black Point: Grain appears darkened at the embryo end. Caused by airborne fungal infection. Harmless and does not affect germination.

There are two conditions affecting barley that anyone growing it should be very aware of. Ignoring these could lead to serious health problems. They are Fusarium Head Blight and Ergot.

Fusarium Head Blight which is also referred to as scab or tombstone is a disease that can contaminate the grain with fungal toxins (mycotoxins). According to the Alberta Ministry of Agriculture's website: "FHB is recognized in the field by the premature bleaching of infected spikelets and the production of orange, spore-bearing structures called sporodochia at the base of the glumes. During wet weather, there may be whitish, occasionally pinkish, fluffy fungal growth on infected heads in the field." FHB develops when there is wet, humid weather during flowering and at the early stages of kernel development. Barley infected with FHB may contain the mycotoxin deoxynivalenol or (DON) which is also known as vomitoxin.

Ergot- this fungal infection mostly affects Rye but can develop on barley. It's easy to detect as the fungus forms Sclerotia which are masses of fungal mycelium that are purple or black in colour and are the same size if not a little bigger than barley grains. If ingested they can cause hallucinations, convulsions, gangrene, abortion, and death. Cool wet Springs that delay pollination and seed development will promote Ergot.

There's not much you can do after a disease hits. Most methods for dealing with fungus or diseases are preventative measures like:

- crop rotation with legumes
- selecting disease resistant varieties
- timing of sowing
- proper plant spacing
- application of fungicide

If you suspect that your barley is infected with FHB it may be a good idea to get it tested. Testing labs are pretty common in grain growing areas. The nice thing about growing on a small scale is that you can visually detect and eliminate any infected looking heads before harvesting. If you see anything black, or moldy and stunted just get rid of it.

Harvesting can be carried out a number of ways depending on the size of your crop and how you plan to thresh the grain. For super small crops of under 500 square feet you can get away with a set of single handed shears to just cut the heads off. Larger plots may require a sickle to cut the straw at the base. For large plots ¼ acre or more a scythe with a cradle attachment is probably the best method. These are available online at various places. What the cradle does is guide the straw into a neat straight pile that's easy to gather. If you're handy I've seen people make cradle type attachments for string mowers but the best and fastest rig that I've seen so far is a push type sickle bar mower with a homemade cradle built onto it. You can see it in action on my blog in the Home Maltsters section. Just look for John's mower.

When to harvest: When you see that the straw just below the seed head has turned yellow it's ok to harvest. Ideally it's best to wait until the straw is very dry but if you see rain in the forecast it's better to harvest a little early to avoid the risk of developing mold or fungus on your grain. Traditionally grain was shooked or stood up in a pile to dry further out in the field as the moisture content must be under 13.5% for proper storage. Drying out the grain is a good practice because the grain separates from the chaff easier and ensures the grain will not get damaged during threshing. I will bring my bins of seed heads inside and wait a month before threshing just to make sure it's all dry.

Dormancy: Newly harvested grain will germinate erratically and this is a problem for maltsters. Before malting, barley must pass through a phase of dormancy. The dormancy phase which is present in many plant species prevents germination prior to the completion of seed maturation. Plant breeders have bred modern barleys to have low levels of dormancy which allows more consistency in the malthouse but are prone to pre-harvest sprouting. The length of time grains remain dormant varies with the weather conditions at harvest and with the barley variety. The method for overcoming dormancy is quite simple. Once grain is dry (between 10-13% moisture) store it in a warm place (25-30C) for 1-2 weeks then reduce temperatures back down to a more ideal storage temperature of 15C 59F.

Threshing and Winnowing

Not as daunting as it sounds. Certainly the old method of beating your grain with a stick is one way to get exercise but it takes a long time. There are better ways. Our goal is to separate the grain from the chaff in a way that doesn't damage the grain.

The best method that I've come across for a small scale operation without much investment is a small length of chain attached to a paint mixer which is attached to a drill. A paint mixer is just a long drill attachment found in the paint department of most hardware stores used to mix paint. I attached 4 small pieces of chain, each about 4 inches long using metal hose clamps. 2 at the base of the mixer and two 4 inches up. The length of the chains and the width of the mixer should equal the width of the bucket.

To use this you will need a 5 gallon bucket with a hole cut in the center of the lid just big enough for the drill attachment about a ½ an inch. Fill the bucket with the heads of the barley up to about a third. Attach the lid and run the drill for about a minute. You might want to wear a dust mask for this. The disadvantage to this system is that it only works with the barley heads and not the straw. The straw will get caught up in the chains.

There are small scale threshers on the market which use pedal power to rotate a drum that has comb like projections sticking out. Imagine a rotating drum covered in nails. While holding the stalks you lay the heads onto the rotating drum and the projections knock off the barley from its stalk. After seeing one in action it doesn't look like it would be that hard to build.

One very low tech method that I've seen also comes from my friend John in Oregon who grows enough barley to make 100 gallons of beer per year. He simply lays out the harvested barley, stalks and all between two tarps and stomps on it, done.

Winnowing. Now we need to separate the chaff from the grain. You could wait for a windy day and throw the grain up in the air several times, which is how it's been done for thousands of years or you can just use a fan. Pour your grain back and forth between two bins and let the fan blow the chaff away. Sometimes I use a tarp to catch the chaff which makes it easier to clean up. I pour back and forth about 7-8 times. Winnowing is important because small bits of straw can encourage mould growth. However, I don't think I've ever winnowed until it's perfectly clean. There are always a few bits of straw and stuff still in there. A lot of this stuff will actually float out when you steep your grain.

Paint mixer thresher.

Feed Barley

Probably the easiest barley to find but the worst to use to make beer. The first time I tried malting at home I used a bag of barley I bought from an animal feed store. I bought their last bag which looked really old but I was too excited to try malting with it to care. Unfortunately, when I first soaked it the water turned dark grey. It was so dirty and full of nasty bits of what looked like mouse turds I ended up throwing it out. I only paid 10 bucks for that 50 lb bag so not a major loss but still it was pretty disappointing.

Using feed barley seems kind of hit and miss. It's super cheap and if you're not growing barley yourself it may be your only option but it's worth it to find a good quality feed barley. I've talked to people who have a good supplier of clean barley but most often you're likely to get barley that includes some "extras" including weed seeds. My advice: wash, wash and wash some more. You may have to rinse it 10 times before the water runs clear.

Aside from the dirt, the first major difference between malting barley and feed barley is that there are strains of barley classified as malting barleys because they have certain genetic qualities that are better for brewing like lower protein and beta glucan amounts as well as higher enzyme levels.

Maltsters are very selective when it comes to the quality of malting barley. So if we ask what makes a good malting barley, then we will find out everything that feed barley is not. Here's a list of factors that make a good quality malting barley. For feed barley expect the opposite!

According to the Alberta Ministry of Agriculture's website, the following characteristics are required in superior malting barley:

Pure lot of an acceptable variety
Germination of 95 per cent or higher (three-day test)
No signs of pre-harvest germination
Protein content of 11 to 12.5 per cent (dry basis)
Moisture content to a maximum of 13.5 per cent
Plump kernels of uniform size
Fully mature
Free from disease
Free of DON mycotoxin caused by fusarium head blight
Free from frost damage
Not weathered or deeply stained
Less than 5 per cent peeled and broken kernels
Free from heat damage
Free of insects, admixtures, ergot, treated seeds, smut and odour
Free of chemical residue
These requirements will affect both the malting and brewing processes, as well as the quality of the end-product, beer.

A note about DON: As previously mentioned, Fusarium head blight is a fungal disease that can appear as a pink or orange colouration or as a black encrustation that's raised and surrounded by white mould. It may even appear after malting has begun. A product of fusarium is the mycotoxin Deoxynivalenol or DON for short. Not only can DON make you sick it can cause gushing in bottled beer. If you see any pink mould or colouration on your grain you might as well throw it out.

Here's a quote from the Ontario Ministry of Agriculture website, what's especially interesting is the last sentence.

DON, also known as vomitoxin, was the principle mycotoxin found in Ontario wheat samples in the 2000 harvest year. Its effects on horses have not been well documented. It is also called vomitoxin because it induces vomiting in pigs and dogs after ingestion of contaminated material. In various livestock species, vomitoxin will cause feed refusal, decreased weight gains, signs of gastrointestinal irritation (e.g., diarrhea, colic, rectal prolapse, and rectal bleeding), reproductive problems, skin irritation, cardiotoxicity and interference with the immune system. In mice, ingestion of DON may cause the overproduction of IgA immunoglobulins in the intestines. IgA accumulates in the kidneys and results in glomerulonephritis (kidney failure). The maximum acceptable concentration of DON in wheat intended for human consumption in flour is 1 ppm. Wheat with a concentration greater than 1 ppm will be diverted for livestock feed.

Just thought I'd throw that in there to cause some panic.

Another toxin which can be found in barley, but is more often found in grains grown in warmer climates is Aflatoxin which in large doses can be lethal. All grain should be stored with a moisture content of less than 13.5% in a cool dry place to avoid molds and fungus from developing.

I also found information on the Government of Canada, Canadian Grain Commission website on how grains are graded which includes information on animal feed. It's nice to know that all grain is tested and regulated to this extent. It does state however that in barley meant for animal feed that .02% excreta is the maximum allowable amount. Yes, it really does say excreta. If I read that right that means that in 50 lb. bag of barley there could be .16 ounces of mouse turds. I'm not sure what .16 ounces of mouse turds looks like, I just hope they float. I do know that .16 oz. is 4.5 grams which is about what a teaspoon of salt weighs. For malt grade barley the number is .01% That's a half teaspoon of turds allowed per 50 lbs.

Finally, if you're still going to try feed barley even after reading this, it's good to know what you're germination rate is so that you can adjust your recipes. The last bag of feed barley I bought had a germination rate of about 80% This means that I ended up with 20% raw unmalted barley in my malt. Make sure to include that in your recipe calculations.

Recipes: Pale Malt

Here are a few kilning schedules that vary widely in the length, from 21 to 84 hours however they all have similar curing temperatures. With a long slow schedule temperatures are very low to start, the roots wither, growth may cease but enzymes continue to develop. This is good for getting a well modified malt that will convert with a single infusion mash. These long schedules were primarily used in England after a long germination. This is why English malt is often described as being more highly modified than continental malt. The reasons for this are worthy of a book which I'll leave to the beer historians.

The first stage in the drying process is called the free drying stage. This is where the moisture easily evaporates from the grain so it's possible to dry with air flow and not much heat 30-40°C 86-104°F. Keeping the temperature low is critical for two reasons. Firstly, enzymes will be activated when the temperature is over 50°C and the moisture content over 10%. Malt must be dried slowly to preserve its diastatic power. In the case of other malts like Munich some sacrifice of the diastatic power will occur since they are kilned at a higher temperature while there is still moisture in the grain. Secondly, At 60°C when the grain has a more than 10% moisture, starch will gelatinize and the malt will not be as friable (important for getting a consistent grind).

During the second stage of kilning at 20% moisture, the kernel and the pores of the husk have shrunk so the water does not escape so easily through the husk. The temperature is raised but the malt temperature is still maintained below 50*C. Airflow can be decreased now to retain heat

At 10% moisture content we can now begin the third phase of kilning which is referred to as the Curing stage and lasts from 3-5 hours. Higher temperatures are needed to evaporate the remaining moisture within the grain. In the case of base malts this is where a lot of the flavour development and colour occurs. This is also where one of the differences between Pale malt and Pilsner malt exists. Ventilation is no longer necessary at this stage in fact the malt does not even have to be on a screen. Curing can be done in your oven on a metal tray.

Here are four recipes for pale malt:

(21-33 hour kilning)
Moisture content 42-45%
Germinate until the starch inside spreads like a chalky paste.
Kiln with ventilation at 35-38°C or 95-100°F until moisture is around 20-25% may be 12-16 hours, depends on airflow.
Raise temperature to 45- 50°C or 113-122°F for 6-12 hours until moisture is 10% or below
Cure at 80-95°C or 176-203°F for 3- 5 hours
Shake off rootlets with a screen or sieve

The following recipes from the American Handy Book of the Brewing Malting and Auxiliary Trades by Robert Wahl and Max Henius. 1902

American malt for Pale Beer: Total time 48 hours
Temperature raised over 10 hours - from ambient to 32°C or 90°F
Raised during the next 4 hours to 49°C or 120°F and maintained for 10 hours
Malt is moved to the lower floor
 Raised over the next 4 hours to 54.5°C or 130°F
Raised over the next 12 hours to 65.5°C or 150°F
Raised over 3 hours to 82°C or 180°F and held for 3 hours
Unloading and recharging the kiln takes 2 hours.

English Malting: Total kilning time (78-84 hours!)
Steeping liquid 10-12°C 50-54°F
Grain depth on floor 2-10 inches. Temp 10-12°C 50-54°F turned every 3-5 hours

Germination takes 10-15 days
"Sprinkling,(with water) if done at all...should not be later than the
fifth or seventh day after the grain has left the cistern (steep tank).
Germination is arrested by withering. Malt is spread very thinly on
the floor to dry out
Kilning depth 4-6 inches
First day 35-38°C 95-100°F
Second day slowly raise to 49°C 120°F
Third day slowly raise to 60-65.5°C 140-150°F
Fourth day raise to 185-200°F 85-93°C for pale malts. 200-230°F
93-110°C for "high dried" malts. Maintain curing temperatures for
at least 5-6 hours.

From a Systematic Handbook of Practical Brewing E.R. Southby
1885
(Total kilning time 84 hours)
"When the malt is once up to 130°F (54.4°C) that temperature
must not be much exceeded until the bulk of the moisture is
expelled and the moisture should be reduced to about six or seven
percent by the time the temperature reaches 140°F (60°C)."
Southby suggests a high starting temperature, bringing it up to
130°F 54.4°C as soon as possible to avoid growth of mould and
bacteria on the malt. He also claims that the diastase is not at risk
at these temperatures.
"About 3-4% more of the moisture should be expelled by the time
the temperature arrives at 155°F (68°C), which should be when
the kiln has been loaded for 60 hours.
Another 12 hours the temperature should have risen to about
175°F (79°C) and then it should be maintained at from 175-185°F
(79-85°C) for the following 12 hours." He is suggesting a long
curing as he was of the opinion that malt should have a final
moisture content of 1.5% or less to ensure longer storage-ability
and better friability for single infusion mashing.

With pale or pilsner malts, studies have shown that storing for 3-4 weeks before using will ensure a higher efficiency when brewing.

Pilsner/ Lager Malt

There are two main differences between lager malt and pale malt. The first is the initial moisture content which for lager malt is between 38-42% and for pale 42-45%. Secondly, the final curing temperatures are lower (63-80°C or 145-176°F) for lager and 79-93°C 175-200°F for pale. In North America more 6-row barley is used for lager malt due to it's higher diastatic power and its greater ability to convert adjuncts but for the home brewing market and in Europe lager malt is often made with 2 row barley.

Having a lower moisture content means that the barley will not grow as much as pale malt and will therefore be less modified. Because of this I would suggest a protein rest in your mash.

Steep 8 hrs. rest 8 hrs and repeat until moisture content is 38-42% (usually takes 3-4 steeps)

Germinate until acrospire is 3/4 the length of the grain and starch becomes chalky when rubbed between your fingers, usually 5-7 days. Keep between 10-13°C (50-55°F) during steeping and 13-15°C (55-59°F) during germination.

Kiln with ventilation at 25-38°C 77-100°F for 12 hrs or more (until grain moisture content has reached 10%). Malt can be dried at room temperature on a screen with a fan for 12-24 hours. Turn often to prevent molds from developing.

Raise temp. to 45- 50°C 113-122°F for 12

hrs Cure at 70-80°C 158-176°F for 3-5 hrs

Here are some more historical examples of pilsner malt schedules taken from variety of sources.

From the *American Handy Book of the Brewing, Malting and Auxilliary Trades* by Robert Wall and Max Henius. These are schedules for a 2 tier malt kiln with both tiers running simultaneously. The grain is loaded into the top tier first and then down to the lower tier closer to the heat. The top tier can then be loaded again while the lower tier is also loaded. This kiln design was primarily used on the continent before being adopted in Britain.

"Kilning American Malt for Extra Pale Beer": total 48 hrs.

Green malt loaded on upper floor of 2 floor kiln.
Temp raised during 10 hours to 32°C or 90°F (malt transferred to lower floor)
Raised during the next 4 hrs to 49°C or 120°F and maintained for 10 hours.
Temp raised over the next 4 hours to 52°C or 125°F
And during the next 12 hours to 54.5°C or 130°F
Then raised within 3 hours to 63°C or 145°F and held for 3 hours.

"Malting in Germany". Malting descriptions taken from Michel's *"Lehrbuch der Bierbrauerei"*

Malt for Bohemian Beer (This may not necessarily be for a pilsner malt as the curing temperatures are pretty high for a light coloured malt but I thought I'd include it anyway)

Moisture 38-42%
Germination room temp. 10-12.5°C or 50-54.5°F 8 inch depth turned every 12 hours when roots develop. Turn every 6-8 hours and spread lower. Max temp. 68°F 20°C
Time of growth 9-10 days
Kilning 24-36 hours

These are last 15 hours of the kilning record, the malt temperatures for the first half in the upper floor are not stated. However the temperatures of the air in the lower chamber are given. These "air-off" temperatures would be the "air on" temperatures for the upper floor. It reads like this:

Hour

1 2 3 4 5 6 7 8 9 10 11 12 13 14 15

Air temp.°F

77 77 81 81 90 95 99 111 117 122 126 131 156 156 156
Malt temp.°F

100 100 113 113 115 117 120 131 144 149 151 153 178 178 178

Same but in Celsius:

Hour	1	2	3	4	5	6	7	8	9	10	11	12	13	14	15
Air in °C.	25	25	27	27	32	35	37	44	47	50	52	55	68	68	68
Malt °C.	38	38	45	45	46	47	49	55	62	65	66	67	81	81	81

Hours 1-12 (of the last 15) As the malt temperature was raised from 37.8 - 67.2°C or 100 - 153° F.   Draft holes open.

Last 3 hours malt temperature at 81.1°C or 178°F Draft holes gradually closed.

Here's the beauty of the two floor system, notice the difference of over 10 degrees centigrade between the malt temperature and the air coming out of the malt bed because the air is saturated. With this schedule the malt on the upper floor would not go over 50°C 122°F during the first twelve hours of malting.

Unfortunately I believe these numbers may be slightly idealized. Normally as the malt gets dryer the difference between the two temperatures decreases. Looking at these numbers you can see that the difference is pretty constant throughout. Whether these were recorded accurately or not doesn't really matter, what's important here are the malt temperatures, these we can use.

As you can see there are a lot of differences between these schedules. Since there are so many factors involved it's best to find out what works for you and your system.

"Pilsen Type Malts and Usual Type" From *La Practique Du Maltage.* Lucien Levy 1898

These malts germinate between 17°- 20°C. 63°-68°F The malt is air dried as much as possible.

Kilned on the upper floor in a bed 12-15 centimeters deep. Temperature is maintained at 31°-33°C 88°-91°F (some maltsters go up to 38°C 100°F)

Malt is turned every hour and stays 15 hours on the upper floor. Vents are left open for the last 3 hours. Moisture is at 8%.

Malt is dropped to the lower floor where it is turned every two hours. Temperature rises to 50°-62.5°C 122°-144.5°F in 12-13 hours and stays at this temperature for two hours for a total of 15 hours on the lower floor.

Historical Malting

During the 1800's the advances in science and technology changed the way malt was produced. The use of the thermometer was standardized by the development of the Fahrenheit scale in 1724 but was slow to be adopted by the brewing industry. Hydrometers began to be employed in 1770 and improvements were made to them in the years that followed. These instruments gave maltsters and brewers scientific insight into their practices. Extract potential and the amount of alcohol produced was now measurable along with exact temperatures so malting and brewing processes could be refined. Also by the late 1700's the manufacturing of coke as a fuel became more efficient and it's transportation became easier through better canal systems and railways. Coke became cheaper and more available and as it was cleaner burning with no smoke flavour being imparted to the flavour of malt it replaced wood and other fuels. In 1873 thanks to French inventor Nicholas Galland pneumatic malting was introduced. Pneumatic refers to forcing cold air through the grain bed which sits on a perforated false floor. Ten years later in 1883 Alphonse Saladin, a former assistant to Galland solved the problem of turning the malt mechanically by inventing the Saladin Box in which the germinating malt is turned by augers that move mechanically from one end of the trough to the other and back again repeatedly on rails. With the use of fans blowing air through the screen at the base of the bed the temperature could be regulated and the malt bed could be much deeper. With the advent of air conditioning in the 1950's malting could be carried out year-round. Fans were also introduced into the malt kiln by the end of the 19th century which sped up the drying process. Many of the kilning schedules I've included here are quite long due to the fact that the kilns relied on their natural draught to draw air up through the malt. In a modern kiln powerful fans blow warm air through the malt allowing the malt bed to be much deeper, up to 4 ft. Before this a kiln bed depth was specific for each kiln but would not often exceed 6".

A cheaper cleaner burning fuel combined with the mechanization of the malting process allowed malt production to expand to a greater scale like everything else during the industrial revolution.

Here's what malting looked like in the early 1800's before many of the significant changes occurred in the industry.

British Floor Malting:

In floor malting the germinating malt is spread on a floor after steeping and turned by hand with shovels. The depth of the malt bed is determined by the maltster and is dependant on the temperature of the respiring malt. At certain times during germination the malt will respire more and produce more heat so the malt would be spread thinner to keep it cool.

The most significant difference between traditional malting and malting today (aside from the physical labour) is how the grain was steeped and the cooler temperatures at which it was germinated. Back then malt was subjected to a continuous steep which would last anywhere from 40-118 hours. The water was changed only a few times if ever. The grain soon becomes stifled as the oxygen is used up in the steep water. This not only causes growth to be delayed but also has the effect of slowing the growth during the germination period. Another contributing factor is that there are substances on the husk of the grain that can inhibit germination. (DeClerck p.131) Repeated changing of steep water washes these away. This is why historically, germination would take 2-3 weeks. The inclusion of air rests during steeping has only been adopted in the last 150 years and has greatly sped up the process of malting. It was suggested by Stopes in 1885 that in Bohemia maltsters had recently adopted a steep schedule that included one air rest. The schedule calls for a steep for 24 hours then drain and let rest for another 24 and finally steeping again but only for 8-10 hours. The water was changed a few times during the steep. It's important to note that in Bohemia and in parts of

Germany that germination was also carried out at much warmer temperatures.

By including oxygen in the steep water and giving the grain air rests, growth starts fast and continues rapidly. It is no wonder that this practice was favoured as it has increased germination speed from 2-3 weeks to less than 1 week. But with rapid growth comes more heat and some would argue a less consistent germination. The low temperatures between 50-55°F (10-12°C) which was typical for English malting will also slow the growth. Today germination is usually carried out between 59-64°F (15-18°C) It's possible that maltsters may have known about the effects of air rests during steeping but avoided such rapid growth with floor malting as it may have been too erratic and produced too much heat to be controlled with shovelling. Once air conditioning and pneumatic malting was introduced and maltsters had the ability to introduce cold moist air into the grain bed, the practice of air rests could be utilized with more control.

In the American Handy Book by Wahl, Henius 1902 pg. 595 when describing floor malting, they state "Growth should not be allowed to proceed too rapidly. The saving of time that might thus be effected is far more than made up for by the fact that an unduly swift development of the acrospire and radicles will not allow of the requisite mellowing of the endosperm which is among the chief objects of germination. Forced growth, therefore, is to be strictly avoided."

It is interesting to note that in one of my experiments malt that was given an air rest did not grow as well at low temperatures (under 10°C) as a malt that was unaerated at the same temperature. The aerated malt started growing faster but stopped short of being fully modified whereas the unaerated malt started later but continued to a greater level of modification.

For nearly 200 years from 1697 to 1880 malting in Britain was bound by taxation laws that dictated the process. Maltsters had to follow rules like minimum steep times and germination times and were fined for not obeying these laws. In 1880 The taxation on malt was abolished. and the malting industry was free to adopt the advancements that sped up the process and reduced the labour costs.

The following procedure has been taken from a report made in 1806 by Thomas, Coventry and Hope. It's one of the first documents containing empirical data including measurements of times, temperatures and malt house conditions, at a time before mechanization, so it's an invaluable source of information.

Malting:

Barley is steeped in square chamber for 40-118 hours, until grain could be crushed end to end between fingers.(Avg. moisture content 42.5 % based on data given)

Scottish maltsters often steeped longer than English. Length of time depended on the original moisture content and the grains ability to absorb water.

Some changed the water once or twice, others not at all

Drained and rinsed (if warm) to wash off slime.

Couch – 16″ deep for 26 hours

Flooring – Spread gradually over time to a depth of 3-4″

Turned 2,3,4, or more times per day depending on conditions

Always kept level thickness to keep temperature even throughout

Sweating – 96 hours (4 days) after casting a rise of 8-12 degrees F usually occurs

During sweating grain becomes wet again for a day or two. (This depends on the humidity of the air, sweating will be less apparent in drier air.)

Temperature must be kept in check by turning.

Temperature of malt at casting 40-50°F. (4.4-10°C) Temp of barn 40-50°F

Temperature of malt at sweat 50-60°F. (10-15.5°C) Temp. of barn 40-50°F

Chitting usually occurs at sweating, but can happen earlier. (Chitting with modern steeping methods which use air resting can occur before or during the final steep. It has been suggested that due to the rapid water uptake that occurs after chitting by the embryo that the endosperm may not get sufficiently hydrated compared to an un-chitted grain although each will show the same moisture content by weight. This may be a contributing factor in the high degree of modification of traditional floor malts)

A day after chitting, the acrospires appear and grow rapidly

Acrospires on 8th day after casting will be half the length of grain, growth then slows.

Grown till acrospires almost reach the end of the grain 12-20 days

Avg. temp. of malt 52-60°F (11-15.5°C) with Scottish being cooler on average than English.

Kiln depth 3-6 inches. (depth of malt bed in kiln)

Kilning starts at body temperature (98.6°F 37°C)

Final curing temperatures recorded ranged from 140-160-170°F. highest observed- 186°F

Suspected some maltsters to kiln up to 212°F for some malts like brown.

40-80 hours on kiln

Pg 33 "Malt may be made brown at a lower temperature for it is not so much the temperature, as the suddenness with which it is raised, while the malt is still moist, which alters the colour."

Here's a kilning schedule for "Malt Anglais" found in La Practique du Maltage Lucien Levy 1898. It refers to a traditional English method for a single floor kiln directly heated with fire. The kilning lasts 3-4 days. The yield is 68-73% of barley weight. (Translated from French)

- At the end of germination wilting is further encouraged by 8-10 hours of shoveling and spreading the bed down to 3-4 centimeters, avoiding a temperature higher than 20°C 68°F. It is then transferred to the kiln.
- Malt temperature raised as fast as possible to 50°C 122°F and is maintained for 12 hours.
- Temperature is raised over another 12 hours to 60°C 140°F.
- Then to 65°, then 70°, 80°, 85° and finally 95° (or in °F 149°, 158°,176°, 185°, 203°) with each increase taking 12 hours. For a total of 84 hours plus however long it took to initially raise the malt temperature to 50°C 122°F
- Malt is turned twice a day blow 70°C 158°F and 3-4 times a day above 70°C 158°F
- If malt has not been wilted it is recommended not to turn it until it is dry (I would assume this means "hand dry" or dry to the touch.)

Modern Malting

Within the last century the amount of time it takes to make malt has gone from two to three weeks to a mere 5-7 days. Perhaps the most significant change has been the addition of air rests during steeping but other methods have been tested and adopted to either reduce time or improve the quality of malt

Recent studies have found steeping schedules that promote a rapid absorption of water and achieve a faster, more uniform growth. Typical steep schedules today are warmer 14-16°C and only include one long air rest between two steeps. A long air rest allows the surface moisture to dry and the grain to absorb more oxygen. After a long air rest the water is absorbed more rapidly in the second steep which is much shorter than the first. However, malt uniformity with a short accelerated schedule is very dependant on the maturity of the grain. Immature grain will lead to inconsistent germination. The length of time grain takes to mature and to overcome it's dormancy can vary with growing conditions, barley variety and storage temperature.

It was discovered in the 1950's that an air rest after the grain has reached 35-37% will overcome water sensitivity and the grain could then be re-steeped to the final 41-46% (Briggs)
Water sensitivity is like dormancy and prevents the grain from chitting when there is surface moisture present. Overcoming water sensitivity means that the grain will chit more evenly.

Among the many additives that have been experimented with to improve efficiency are limewater, hypochlorites, sodium hydroxide, and hydrogen peroxide. Two additives in common use are Gibberellic acid, a growth hormone that is naturally present in barley and Potassium bromate which is used to reduce the heat output of the respiring grain.

Other techniques used to speed up or improve the process are abrasion of the grain as well as the squeezing of partly steeped grain for more rapid water absorption. Spray-steeping and steep aeration are two techniques that have been around for at least a hundred years but have had varying results which could be due to other factors such as grain maturity.

One method that is in common practice and was scientifically proven as early as 1909 which you can use at home is carbon dioxide extraction. Since CO_2 is heavier than air it will sit in the grain bed and has the effect of slowing the growth. If malt is on a screen or perforated tray, fans can be used to suck the CO_2 down through the bed.

Since I'm in no rush to malt my grain saving time is not a priority for me, also these results may be impossible without the use of gibberellic acid and other additions. Included is a schedule from an actual malting company as well as a proposed schedule with a warm steep (Muller, Methner 2015) which saves even more time, but incredibly did not raise the levels of DON in their tests results. Some disadvantages with the accelerated malting schedule observed in their study were slightly decreased extract value by .5 -1.5% owing to a higher pH and a slightly lower diastatic power. Advantages aside from the obvious time savings include a reduction in proteolytic modification, higher oxidative flavour stability, higher malt homogeneity and improved cytolytic modification. (Beta-glucan degradation). Another advantage was less DMS-P (dimethyl sulfide precursor) which could mean less kilning and boiling time is needed to reduce the DMS-P content in the malt or wort.

Industrial Malting eg.

Steeping:
1st steep 4 hours at 14°C 57°F
Air rest 15 hours at 16°C 61°F
2nd steep 2 hours at 14°C 57°F

Germination: (total time 125 hours)
24 hours at 18°C 64°F
24 hours at 16°C 61°F
77 hours at 15°C 59°F

Industrial malting continued.
Kilning: (total time 18.5 hours)
1 hour 60°C 140°F
12 hours 65°C 149°F
1 hour 70°C 158°F
1 hour 75°C 167°F
1 hour 80°C 176°F
2.5 hours 84°C 183°F
Total time start to finish 165 hours

Accelerated malting procedure (Muller, Methner)
Steeping:
1st steep 5.5 hours at 22°C 72°F
Air rest 18 hours at 21°C 70°F
2nd steep 1.25 hours 20°C 68°F

Germination: (total time 74 hours)
8 hours 20°C 68°F
24 hours 21°C 70°F
42 hours 20°C 68°F

Kilning: (total time 24 hours)
6.5 hours 37.5°C 99.5°F
4.5 hours 40°C 104°F
2.5 hours 45°C 113°F
2 hours 50°C 122°F
2 hours 55°C 131°F
1.5 hours 60°C 140°F
4 hours 80°C 176°F
1 hour 82°C 180°F
Total time start to finish 123 hours

Vienna Malt

Vienna malt is a base malt that is less sweet than pale malt and slightly darker with more toasted flavours. Vienna malt starts out as a pilsner malt but is kilned slightly darker than pale. 3-4 Lovibond D.P. 80.

It took me a while to find a good description of Vienna malt. This one is from the American Handy Book of the Brewing Malting and Auxiliary Trades by Robert Wahl and Max Henius 1902.

There are three differences between Pale malt and Vienna. First of all Vienna starts with a lower moisture content at 38-42%, like a lager malt. Pale malt is typically 42-44%.(Although I have since seen a recipe for Vienna that started with a 44-46% moisture content, the rest was pretty much the same as this one.) It also has a slightly warmer germination during the last 4 or 5 days. A warmer germination will promote the development of proteolytic enzymes, the enzymes which act on protein. According to the Handy book the last 5 days of a 10 day germination for Vienna is no higher than 19°C or 66°F but the example given does go up to 20°C. Pale malt is typically germinated at 15-18°C 59°F-64°F or cooler in the example of English malting. 10 days is a long time to germinate and is only possible with an un-aerated steep (see historical malting) If you're using an aerated steep you can extend the germination time by spreading it thin to wilt the roots, this will slow the growth of the acrospire. Vienna malt is then kilned at a low temperature until it's at what I'm going to assume is a 10% moisture content and then cured at increasing temperatures up to 212°F 100°C for the last hour. So a little hotter than pale which is cured at 176-194°F 80-90°C. I often see Vienna malt lumped together with Munich malt in descriptions of malts but judging by this process it's much closer to pale malt than Munich. Munich malt is more highly modified, it starts with a much higher moisture content. It's also germinated at warmer temperatures which reach 25°C 77°F and when kilned the temperature is raised while there is still a certain amount of moisture in it.

Here are my notes from the book:

Steeping Period: 57-84 hours (continuous steep, no air rests)
Moisture 38-42 % Couch temp. No higher than 66°F or 19°C for
the last 5 days

Germination period 9-10 days malt never allowed to mat. Depth
4.5-7 inches
Temperature not to exceed 59°F 15°C when rootlets are
developing (first 1-2 days)

Floor record example: (8 day total germination)

Temp. Day 1 50-57°F 10-14°C 7- 6.3 inches deep

Day 2 57-63.5°F 14-17.5°C 6-5.5 inches deep

Day 3 66-68°F 19-20°C Next 5 days temp maintained at 68°F or
20°C 4.7-5.5 inches deep. Turned every 6-8 hrs. Never allowed to
mat.

Kilning: 24 hrs.

The malt is loaded on the upper floor at 95-100°F 35-38°C all
draughts being open until it is "air-dry" Unfortunately, it does not
state what the moisture content is at this point.
"The draught is checked and temperature raised to 144-156°F
62-69°C"

The last 12 hours of malt temperatures go like this: 110.75°F
43.75°C, 117.5°F 47.5°C, 122°F 50°C, 140°F 60°C, 149°F 65°C,
156°F 69°C, 171°F 77°C, 185°F 85°C, 200°F 93°C, 202°F 95°C,
212°F 100°C.

Toasted Malts
Victory, Biscuit and Amber

These are the lightly roasted malts that start as pale or pilsner malts and are roasted to varying degrees. They also vary between the companies that make them. They contribute a toasty or cracker like flavour to a beer. Some people recommend soaking the malt for an hour before toasting claiming that it makes the malt sweeter but I have found that the grain does not re-hydrate enough to affect the inside of the malt and that it really doesn't stew for long enough to actually work. What soaking does do is delay any burning that would occur at a high temperature, at least until it's dry. The end result is that soaked malt that's toasted just until dry at a high temperature has the same flavour of un-soaked malt that's been toasted at a low temperature (like at 250°F), so it's not really worth doing. I've listed the drying times of a soaked malt anyway if you want to try it.

I've also included a schedule for Amber malt listed in the book Malt and Malting by Henry Stopes published in 1885. If starting from a pale malt the last four hours of this recipe will create a malt similar to a store bought amber malt. The recipe does go up to 250°F so there would be a significant loss of diastatic power. Amber malts made before the use of Black Patent malt in 1817 would have been kilned at a slightly lower temperature.

Before the early 1800's when malts were referred to as either pale, amber, or brown, all three would have varying levels of diastatic power, but would have had enough to be used individually. It's safe to say that Amber would not have been kilned above 212°F in order to maintain diastatic power. Evidence for this can be found in The Scotch Bigg report of 1806 by Thomas, Coventry and Hope who state that the highest temperature they observed during their reporting was 186°F but suspected that higher temperatures may have been used, up to 212°F. The idea to use black patent malt as a colouring and flavour agent opened the door to the development of other specialty malts using higher temperatures since maintaining diastatic power was no longer an issue as long as the specialty malt was used in small amounts and in conjunction with pale malt.

Biscuit:
From pale malt
250°F for 1 hour **or**
300°F for 30 min **or**
350°F for 20 min

Victory and Amber:

250°F for 1 1/2 to 2 hours **or**
300°F for 45 minutes **or**
350°F for 30 minutes **or**
If soaked for 1 hour 350F for 45 minutes (or just until it's dry)

Amber Malt: From Malt and Malting: An Historical , Scientific and Practical Treatise. H Stopes 1885 p. 159-161

Germinates as a pale malt

Kilning: First 12 hrs. below 80°F 26.6°C
End of hour 18 85°F 29.4°C
End of hour 20 125°F 51.6°C
"   21 140°F 60°C
"   22 160°F 71°C
"   23 180°F 82°C
"   24 200°F 93°C
"   25 220°F 104.4°C
"   26 240°F 115.5°C
"   26.5 250°F 121.1°C

Stopes also recommends that the final curing stage (last 5-6 hrs) can be carried out with dry beechwood in the kiln for the best flavour.

The version seen in my Youtube video started with a finished pale malt and kilned at 200°F for 1 hr. 220°F for 1 hour 240°F for an hour then 250°F for an hour.

The Melanoidin Family
Aromatic, Munich, and Melanoidin Malts
Brumalt

Here's a group of malts that deserve their own category. They are sometimes referred to as "high kilned" malts and in some old text books they're referred to simply as "darker malts" which can be confusing because they're not necessarily referring to dark roasted malts like chocolate malt. They're referring to Munich, Aromatic and Melanoidin malt. Brumalt is also referred to as a Melanoidin malt. These malts differ from pale and lager malt in that they have a higher initial moisture content (resulting in a higher degree of modification), they're germinated at warmer temperatures and they're kilned differently- warmer sooner and at certain points without ventilation. The goal when making these malts is to produce a rich malt with a strong aroma. Different companies have slightly different schedules but they all have the same objective- to produce melanoidins.

Melanoidins are reddish-brown coloured substances which contribute the characteristic rich bready, malty aroma and flavour. These are also what give bread crust it's colour and flavour and are produced as a result of Maillard reactions. Maillard reactions occur in all malts to a certain degree (except in air dried "wind" malt). However, in other malts like biscuit for example they occur when the malt is in a dry state. In "melanoidin" malts it occurs when the malt is still moist. Using the bread analogy again, a bread's crust is formed in the oven from the wet dough, as it cooks. The crust develops it's own unique flavour. Whereas, if you toasted a slice of that cooked bread you would get browning but with a different flavour, a toast flavour. This also holds true for malt.

Actually each step in the production of these malts promotes these reactions. Firstly they are steeped until they have a moisture content of 45-48%. During germination the malt is allowed to reach 20-25°C for Munich and Aromatic or higher for Melanoidin and Brumalt as opposed to 15-18°C for pale and lager malt. These higher temperatures promote the development of proteolytic enzymes, the enzymes which act on protein. The protein in the malt is then degraded by these enzymes during the higher initial kilning or at 50°C or 122°F into peptides, polypeptides and amino acids. This is done while the grain still contains moisture and is akin to the idea of stewing for crystal malt only at the "protein rest" temperature range to target the action of these enzymes. There is also the formation of sugars occurring during the malting process (aided by the high modification) and when combined with amino acids and heated at the higher curing temperatures produce Melanoidins. This is what's called the Maillard reaction named after the French chemist who discovered this in 1913.

Munich Malt

Here are six different methods for making Munich malt, all from different sources. The first method is how I've made Munich with my kiln. As you can see it has the shortest kilning due to the small amounts being dried. It probably should be done over a longer period of time, I would suggest letting the malt wilt at room temperature for a day before kilning.

All of these methods are similar in that they all start with a high moisture content, have a warm germination and are well modified. For the first four methods the initial kilning is long with limited ventilation during which time reducing sugars and amino acids accumulate. (Briggs).

In the stewing phase temperatures increases vary from 60-75°C 140-167°F when there is between 15-25% moisture. Given the small amount of moisture and the temperature range there will be a small amount of conversion happening within the malt. Curing temperatures are high and also vary with each method from 185-250°F 85-121°C

Aromatic malt at 20 L it is often considered to be the same as a dark Munich. To achieve this one simply has to cure at a slightly higher temperature. However, one malting company calls their Aromatic malt an Aromatic/melanoidin malt. Perhaps in this case a different schedule is employed that incorporates more stewing at lower temperatures. Something maybe in-between a Munich and Melanoidin malt. If there is more stewing in the higher 60-75°C range with a higher moisture content than 25% then you start crossing into the caramel malt territory which is not where Aromatic malt lies. As you can see below there are a lot of variations for Munich malt.

Method # 1 (24 hour kilning)

Steep until moisture content is 47-48% (8 hrs soaking, 8 hrs. air rest) at 10-15°C (50-59°F)

Germinate at 15-18 degrees until acrospire reaches 1/3 to ½ the length of grain, 4-5 days. Bring inside at 20°C (68°F).

Allow acrospire to reach the full length of the grain and grain temperature to reach 25°C (77°F)

Kiln with limited ventilation on screens gradually increasing temperature up to 50°C 122°F (malt temp.) for 16 hrs or until moisture is down to 20-25%
Stewing: Raise temperature to 60-65°C 140-149°F (malt temperature) with little to no ventilation for 4-6 hours then open vents and continue at this temperature for a few more hours until moisture is under 10%
Can be cured at 185-200°F 85-93°C 3-5 hrs. for a light Munich. For a darker Munich cure between 220-235°F 104-113°C for 3 hours.

Method # 2 This method is based on information from La Practique Du Maltage (Levy 1897-1898)

Use a continuous un-aerated steep which could last up to 110 hours, changing the water a few times (perhaps once a day) until the moisture content is high (46-48%)

Germinate until the acrospires are the full length of the grain and the rootlets are between 1.5 and 2 times the length of the grain. Temperature of the malt does not exceed 20-21°C 68°-70°F and the malt is allowed to felt. Malt is broken up and spread out to wilt

before kilning. Duration of malting (using an un-aerated steep) will be 10-11 days.
Some barley will not endure the long steep necessary for Munich malt. In this case steep for 60 hours and spray at each turning (not in between) until the rootlets are ¾ the length of the grain.

Kilning: (36-48 hours)
 Malt bed is 24 cm. deep at 38°C 100°F with a slow stream of air.
Malt is turned every three hours after four hours on the upper floor. Vents are open until two thirds of the time it spends on the upper floor have passed.
The vents are then closed little by little until they are less than a quarter open by the end of the upper floor kilning.
When moisture content has dropped to 15% malt is dropped to the lower floor and temperature is increased to 75°C (167°F) and held for 12 hours. (This temperature is pretty high and I would assume that this is the "air-on" temperature.)
Cured at 189.5-212°F (87.5-100°C) for 2 hours.
Vents on the lower floor are wide open for the first quarter, half closed until the last third of the operation, then closed until the end.
The problem with this schedule is the obvious lack of times. It also neglects to state what the malt temperature is at the time it is dropped which is probably higher than 38°C since the vents are now almost closed. My guess is that it would take maybe 4 hours for the malt temperature to reach 75°C making the total 18 hours for the lower floor and 18- 30 on the upper floor.

Method # 3 (48 hour kilning) Wahl and Henius 1902

From the American Handy Book of the Brewing Malting and Auxiliary Trades by Robert Wahl and Max Henius published in 1902 in which they reference Leyser-Heiss and Michel's "Lehrbruch der Bierbrauerei"

General malting instructions:

Steep water 9-12.5°C 48-54.5°F renewed every 12 hrs. Under unfavorable circumstances the water should be renewed every 6-8 hrs.
Floor depth 11.8-19.7 inches. Turned every 12 hrs.
Maximum temp.of grain bed 21-22.5°C 70-72.5°F
Germination period 6-8 days then spread to a depth of 2 inches to wither.

Munich:

Bavarian (Munich): 44-45 % moisture. Steep temp. 12.5°C 54.5°F time of steeping 90-120 hours (continuous steep - no air rests just water changes)

Floor depth 8-10 inches turned every 12 hrs. Or more depending on temp.

5-6th day allowed to lie 15-18 hrs in order to mat. Generally malt is allowed to mat twice and the temperature allowed to rise to 22°C 72°F

Temp. of germination room at 9-10°C 48-50°F and the temp. of grain rises gradually on its own over the germination period.

Kilning:

This is for a two tier kiln, the air temperatures in the kiln above the malt bed are given, which are referred to as the "air-off" temperatures. Temperatures below the malt bed are the "air-on" temperatures which would be much warmer. The actual malt temperature would be somewhere in between.

Upon reaching upper floor moisture is between 37-40%

Upper floor 24hrs - Temperatures not stated

Lower floor 12 hrs at 40-44°C 104-111°F (Air-off temperature "Air-on" would be approximately 55-65°C. Malt temperature perhaps 45-50°C)

Moisture now down to 20-24% and drafts or dampers then closed.

Raised over 6 hrs to 56-60°C 133-140°F (this is the final air-off temp. after the 6 hours) or until moisture is 10-14%

(Curing:) Temp. then raised for 3 hrs held for last 3 hrs. Air temp in kiln (air-off temp.) rises gradually from 60-84°C 140-183°F

Temperature in the malt during these last 6 hours goes from 82-106°C 180–223°F. (Quite a difference from the air-off temperature.)

The air-on temperatures for the lower floor are included for the last 6 hrs. They go from 97-121°C 207-250°F for the first 3 and then maintained at 250°F or 121°C for the last 3.

Moisture down to 5-6% Finished malt (after cooling) 1.5-2%

Method #4 (48 hour kilning) Kunze.

Another schedule for a two-floor system in Technology Brewing and Malting by Wolfgang Kunze which includes time, malt temperature and moisture content for the upper and lower floors.

Time	Malt temp.°C Upper Lower floor floor		Moisture content Upper Lower floor floor			Operation of turners after (h)	Damper operation	
1-4	20°		44%				1-10	open
5-9	30°		30%			Every 2 hours		
10-14	40°		25%				11-14	¼ shut
15-19	60°		22%				14-17	½ shut
20-24	65°		20%			Every 1 hour	19-23	shut
25-29		50°		16%		Every 1 hour	25-34	open
30-34		50°		12%				
35-39		65°		7%		Every 1 hour	35-38	¼ shut
40-44		90°		5%			38-41	½ shut
							41-43	¾ shut
45-48		105°		3%		Continuous	43-47	shut

The graph below is from the latest fifth edition of Technology, Brewing and Malting. There's a slight variance in the temperatures, with the older chart, finishing the top floor and starting the bottom floor at slightly higher temperatures, but both of these will still make Munich malt.

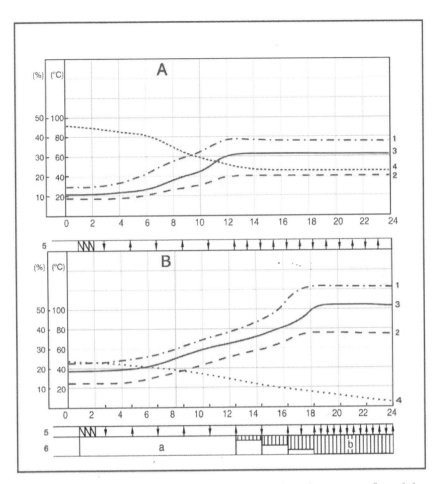

Fig. 2.89 Withering and kilning schema for dark malt in a two-floor kiln (according to Narziß)
(A) Upper floor, (B) lower floor
(1) Temperature below the floor, (2) temperature above the floor, (3) temperature in the malt, (4) water content in the malt, (5) turning, (6) drafts a = open, b = closed

Note: Although not stated in the graph, vent schedule (6) would apply to the upper floor as well.

Method #5 Henry Stopes description of malting in Bavaria 1885

Stopes describes the "warm sweat" method of germination that was practiced in Bavaria and in some other parts of Germany. (pg.342) "After steeping, the corn is kept for two or even three days in a comparatively shallow couch of five or six inches, where it is turned at least twice every tide. (12 hours) When chitting begins, the depth of the couch is greatly increased (generally doubled), and allowed to gather heat rapidly. It is only turned when the surface becomes dry. After about two days, the depth is constantly increased until the finish, when it is not unusual to find it so much as 24 inches deep, and upwards of 100° (38°C) in temperature."

Kilning "...dried by loading the kiln fairly thick (about 8 inches) when it is air dried by means a tolerably strong current of air at 88°Fahr. (31°C); Unfortunately the moisture contents are not stated but there is a description on pg. 384 that reads "For Bavarian beers-that is to say those having palatefulness, the temperature is raised above 111° Fahr. (44°C), when the grain is hard but not quite dry." "the ventilators are then closed, and heat with little air allowed to pass through the grain, so that the temperature, in the course of a couple of hours, rises to about 170° Fahr. (76.7°C) when the desired cooking processes are completed. The resulting darkening of the endosperm has been but little studied." Stopes suggests that there is a "natural caramelisation of starch, when still moist at such temperature." "After drying in this way, (5-6 hours) the air -passages still being kept closed, the temperature is raised to 190° Fahr. and is kept drying off for two or three hours at least. At this temperature the malt-aroma is produced."

Method #6 (36 hour kilning) Petit 1904

This schedule is found in Brasserie and Malterie by Paul Petit 1904. It has a very fast initial drying phase and it's safe to assume fans were being used in order to dry the malt this fast. Unfortunately we don't know the rate at which the temperature rose in the second stage so this schedule is not very helpful other than showing us the variety of schedules used to make Munich malt.

Malt is loaded on the upper floor to a depth of 20-25 cm.
Ventilation with a strong current of air at 25-30°C 77-86°F for 6-8 hours. After which moisture is down to 15-18%
Vents closed (fans off) and temperature is allowed to rise over 18-24 hours to 167-176°F 75-80°C
Temperature raised to 203-212°F 95-100°C for 3-4 hours
230-239°F 110-115°C for darker malt.

Melanoidin/ Brumalt

This malt takes the idea of protein stewing a step further. Like Munich it starts out with a high moisture content and is well modified. During the end of germination temperatures are encouraged to reach up to 50°C or 122°F during which time a lot of preformed sugars and amino acids are produced. Traditionally this was achieved by stacking the malt and covering it with a tarp for about 36 hours. Respiration causes the stack to heat up and produce carbon dioxide. With such warm temperatures and low oxygen levels lactobacillus bacteria, which is already present on the husk multiplies rapidly and lowers the pH of the malt giving it a touch of sourness. On a small scale achieving these temperatures is only possible by either using an insulated cooler and allowing the malt to heat up by itself or by sealing the malt in a ziploc bag cutting off all oxygen and adding heat. The malt does need oxygen in order to respire and heat up so if you're using the cooler method do not seal it with a lid. Instead, cover it with towels or something that will allow some oxygen but preserve the heat.

Honey malt is produced by the Gambrinus Malting Company and according to their website is a type of Brumalt. However, their malt undergoes other steps in its production which is their trade secret. As the name suggests Honey malt tastes like honey but also has an almost vinous character to it. The flavour is unique and stronger than the Melanoidin malts that I've tried, the pH is a little lower but the colour is similar in the 20-30L range.

This recipe will give you a sweet yet slightly sour malt at about 30L. Because of its lower kilning temperatures it retains some diastatic power.

Steep until 48%
Germinate for at least 6 days at 13°C, when acrospires are at 3/4 bring up to room temperature. (acrospires on average are now the full length of grain)

Couch (lactic acidification phase) in a zip-loc bag sealed for 16 hours at 37°C. For Melanoidin malt which is less sour than Honey malt decrease time to 8 hours or take out of sealed bag at a certain point.
ramp up temp to 50°C (proteolysis phase) and hold for 8-10 hours for about a 30L colour, Add more time for more colour 16-18 hrs = around 60L. Or hold for only 2-4 hours for a lot less colour.

Natural method:
If using the natural method put malt into an insulated box or cooler near the end of germination (acrospires are at 75%) and cover with towels or something insulative.
 Temperature should climb up towards 50°C. Kiln when temperature starts to drop or after 36 hours.
Kiln at 40-45°C for 24 hours or until moisture is below 10%
Cure:
1 hour at 175°F 79°C
1 hour at 185°F 85°C
3 hours at 190°C 88°C

Caramel Malts

Caramel malt is made by stewing green malt (germinated grains that have not yet been kilned) at 149-158°F 65-70°C. The grains undergo an "in-house" mashing. After a few hours saccharification occurs and the endosperm liquefies into a syrup.

The difference between Crystal malt and Caramel malts are that Crystal have been stewed and roasted in a drum which is a more effective way of achieving the conversion of starches to sugar. Caramel malts are usually made in a kiln and are therefore not as consistent, some grains convert more than others depending on the location in the grain bed. When making caramel at home on such a small scale it's pretty easy to get a consistent results and almost all of the kernels will have a "glassy" candy-like interior.

Start with a very well modified green malt (moisture 45-48%) on a tray and cover with tin foil. I prefer a tray instead of a pot because I find that with the grain spread out, the heat is more evenly distributed. Heat the malt between 149-158°F 65-70°C for 3-4 hours or until the syrup is evident when the malt is squeezed between your fingers. It's important to use a probe thermometer to measure the temperature of the malt as it may take two hours or longer to get up to the right temperature.

Some texts include a proteolytic phase in their schedules but only when making dark caramels because this step will add more colour. This step should be skipped when making cara-pils or dextrin malt which are the lightest of the caramel malts. These can also be made with less modified malt. During the last 30-36 hours of germination allow the temperature to reach 45-50°C 113-122°F. Alternatively stew in the kiln covered with foil at 45-50°C 113-122°F for 3-4 hours before raising the temperature again to Saccharification temperatures. This step ensures the enzymatic breakdown of proteins.

Total kilning time: 12 hours.
Hour 1: 149°F 65°C covered
Hour 2: Increased to 158°F 70°C covered
Hours 3 to 5 -158°F 70°C until signs of liquefication
Covers removed and malt put on screens to dry
For Dextrin or Cara-Pils dry at 131-140°F 55-60°C until its
moisture content is 6-7%
For all other Caramels dry for 3 hours at 158°F 70°C or until
moisture is down to 10-20%
For a light Caramel (15L) Cure at 200°F (93°C) for 3 hours
otherwise skip this step.
Increase temperature to 225°F (107°C) for 3 hours.
Temp. increased to 250°F (121°C) 30 minutes = (20-25L)
1 hour at 250°F (121°C) = approx. 60L
1 1/2 hours at 250°F (121°C) = approx. 100L
2 hours at 250°F (121°C) = approx. 140L

Special B Type Malt

I love this malt. I don't think any other malt adds as much distinct character to a beer than Special B. A great malt to use for Belgian Dubbels with it's sweet raisiny flavours, this malt is essentially a dark caramel which utilizes a "protein stew" at 50°C 122°F before the "saccharification stew" at 65-70°C 149-158°F. Kilning at a lower temperature than normal caramel avoids any roasty flavours. Most of the dark colour and unique flavour is coming from the melanoidin production during the protein stew. Use up to 10% in dark ales or try small amounts in lighter ales. The colour is about 120L.

Steep to a moisture content of 45%. Germinate at 15°C 59°F

Bring inside to room temperature when acrospire = ¾ length of the grain.

Last 24-36 hrs of germination at room temperature until average acrospire length = full length of grain.

Place on a tray covered with tin foil for 12-16 hrs. at 50°C 122°F

Increase temperature to 65-70°C 149-158°F (malt temp.) for 4 hours (still covered)

Put onto a drying screen in the oven at 200°F (93°C) for 5 1/2 hours.

Making Caramel malt from Pale malt

This is worth a try if you don't have access to raw barley or caramel malt. Unlike a lot of recipes I've read, this one has a very long stewing phase which I believe is necessary to achieve conversion with a pale malt as it has less diastatic power than malt in its green state.

Steep pale malt using an absorption method that is, adding almost the same weight of cold water (less 5% that's already in the malt) so that over the course of 24 hours the grain will absorb this water giving it about a 50% moisture content. This way there's no risk of washing away any enzymes or sugars that are in the malt. Keep cool until the water has been absorbed.

Put malt on a baking tray and cover with tin foil. Stew at 65-70°C 149-158°F for 8 hours. Note: it may take 4 hours to get the malt to this temperature for a total of 12 hours stewing. Be sure to measure the temperature in the malt bed. To test for conversion squeeze a kernel. If some clear liquid comes out then it's ok to dry. Some starchy goop with the clear liquid is also ok, but if it's all starchy goop then continue stewing.

Once malt has liquified inside, then dry on a screen at 70°C 158°F for 12 hours.

Raise temperature to 200°F 93°C for an hour for about 10L **or**

Cure at 250°F 121°C for an hour to get about 30L

1 ½ hours at 250°F 121°C for 60L

Roasted Malts
Chocolate, Roasted Malt, Roasted Barley

These malts also start as pale malts and can be made with store bought pale or pilsner malt. Different malts may give you slightly different results. For example a 6-row malt with a higher protein content may give you a slightly different colour and flavour compared to a 2-row pale malt. I usually roast small amounts of 1 or 2 pounds so that my roasted malts are always fresh. It is my personal opinion that roasted malts should be used as soon as possible but everyone's taste is different. Some people suggest waiting for the "harsh" flavours to fade, but I haven't experienced any harsh flavours immediately after roasting. I find there to be a deeper, bolder and less stale flavour. Like roasting coffee, the fresher the better. This is not the case with base malts where it's been proven in studies that after three weeks from kilning, lautering improves. My method is to roast the malt between two cookie trays to distribute the heat as evenly as possible. Stir every 15 minutes or so. I've seen plenty of other ways people have roasted malt including using a bar-b-que rotisserie as well as a portable electric rotisserie. These are excellent ideas as you can roast outside. Roasting malt creates a lot of smoke so roasting outside is a good idea. If you're inside be prepared, your fire alarm will go off. It's also a good idea to have a fire extinguisher handy in case the barley catches fire.

In Wolfgang Kunze's Technology of Brewing and Malting he describes the practice of wetting the malt before roasting. This is carried out in the roasting drum by spraying water at 158-176°F 70-80°C for 1 ½-2 hours while the drum is rotating until there is a moisture content of 10-15%. Soaking the grains like this will encourage the Maillard reaction and will affect the colour as well as adding a slight caramelization to outer layer of the malt. Some authors suggest simply soaking the grain for 1 hour in water for a similar effect. However, when malting at home on a small scale I think adding water can be detrimental to your malt. At these high temperatures the water will instantly turn to steam and speed up the cooking process so you run a greater risk of charring your malt sooner than if you did not use water. If you do use water just shorten the times given and keep a close eye on it near the end.

Chocolate: Store bought chocolate malts range in colour from 200L to 500L. This recipe makes a malt in the 350-450L range. Roast at 400°F (204°C) for 1 to 1 ½ hours, stir every 15 minutes.

Black Patent Malt: Roast at 375°F (190°C) for one hour then 30 min at 450°F (232°C)
Or roast at 400°F (204°C) for 2-21/2 hours stirring every 15 min.

Roasted Barley: Roast at 450-480°F (232-249°C) for 1 hour turn every 15 minutes. Or for more control roast at 400-425°F (204-218°C) for 2 hours stirring every 15 min.

Of course you can experiment with these times and temperatures, what you're looking for is a malt that is uniform in colour and not charred. You'll know when it's charred as it looks completely black and turns to dust when crushed between your fingers, basically it looks like charcoal. This means you've roasted too long or are too hot.

Debittered Black Patent Malt

With the availability of hulled barley, and hulless barley you can make any of your malts "debittered" since most of the astringent and bitter flavours come from the husk. Hulled barley is raw barley with most of the husk removed mechanically. Whereas, Hulless barley refers to varieties of barley that lose their husk when threshed like modern wheat. Both will sprout and can be used for malting. These are not to be confused with pearl barley which is processed even further to have all the outer layers removed. The problem that arises from malting hulled barley is that like wheat the acrospire is unprotected and can easily break off killing the grain. It's important to turn the germinating grain carefully.

Ideally you're going to want to cook this malt outside. Also one last warning, as with all roasted malts the smell is pretty strong and will last a couple of days, so if you don't like the smell of coffee roasters you won't like the smell of roasting malt either. I recommend using the rotisserie function on a bar-b-que if you have one. You can make a miniature drum out of a large metal can. If you can find a lid for it great, I found a small cake pan with straight sides that fit over a coffee can to act as a lid but otherwise you can make one out of tin, it doesn't have to be pretty it just has to keep the grain inside. I've also seen people use a metal box instead, that way you don't need a baffle inside to stir the grain like you would need with a drum shape.

An alternative to the bar-b-que would be a small rotisserie which you can see on pioneering home malster tlgrimmy's youtube channel. These work well and you find them in thrift stores usually for under $30 just make sure it's able to get hot enough - up to 450 degrees F. (232°C)

If you decide to make black malt inside your house I find the fastest way to make it in your oven is to put no more than 2 pounds between two oven trays. This will distribute the heat evenly but you still need to stir the malt every 15 minutes. Black malt was often sprayed with water at the end of kilning to halt the kilning process. It was also sprayed to prevent the malt from igniting. I find that when I spray with water I have a less consistent roast, I think it causes uneven heat distribution with the small amount of grain I use so I don't do it.

Steep at 10°C 50°F till 42-45 % moisture, for hulless barley this only takes 1 - 8 hr steep plus a 2nd 2 - 4 hour steep with an 8 hour air rest in between.
Germinate at 15°C 59°F until acrospire is ¾ or starch is pasty when rubbed between fingers.
Kiln at 35-40°C 95-104°F for 12 hours or until moisture is below 10% Or dry for 24 hrs at room temperature with a fan, until moisture is less than 10% Hulless barley dries faster the regular barley. Drying times may vary depending on your climate.
Curing for 5 hours at 185°F (85°C)
Roast at 375°F (190°C) for 1 hour stirring every 15 min.
Then 450°F (232°C) for 30 minutes
Times may vary depending on the size of your barley kernels and actual oven temperatures.

Brown Malts

Here's where malting at home has advantages, you can make malts that no longer exist like diastatic brown malt. In England before 1817 (the year Black Patent Malt was introduced) there were three types of malt, pale, amber and brown. Of course these would vary between maltsters but all were meant to retain enough diastatic power to be used by themselves but were often used in combination. In the early 1800's brewers realized the economic advantage of using Black Patent malt in combination with pale malt since the diastatic power of brown malt was lower. As coke became a better choice to fuel malt kilns since it became cheaper and cleaner burning than wood traditional brown malt faded out of use. Some of my first failed attempts at producing diastatic brown malt made one of the best pale ales I've ever made even though I was trying to make a porter. After that beer I vowed to dry all of my malts over fire, it can add a nice touch of smoke, not as much as you might think, definitely not like a rauchbier. The smokeyness depends on how clean your fire is burning.

I know of three different malts referred to as Brown malt which causes a lot of confusion among readers of historical recipes and texts. There is traditional brown, blown malt, and modern brown. Here's my attempt to distinguish the different types.

Diastatic brown malt - A dark malt kilned over a fire fueled with coal, wood or straw which has enough diastatic power to convert itself. Made during a time before the widespread use of thermometers and hydrometers the colours and level of diastatic power would have varied between maltsters. An essential source of information on malts of this time comes from the London and Country Brewer by William Ellis published in 1736.
What I find most interesting is that the description given for the production of malt includes a 36 hour couch before it is kilned, a practice that is used in the production of Munich type malts. Page 7-8 describes "When it is at this degree and fit for the Kiln, (wilted

or when "the Root begins to be dead") it is often practised to put it into a Heap and let it lye twelve Hours before it is turned, to heat and mellow, which will much improve the malt if it is done with moderation and after that time it must be turned every 6 hours during twenty four; but if it is overheated, it will become like Grease and be spoiled, or at least cause the Drink to be unwholesome; when this Operation is over, it then must be put on the Kiln to dry four, six, or 12 hours according to the nature of the malt. The pale sort requires more leisure and less fire than the amber or brown sorts." Even though the temperature of the heap was not measured we do know that by including this step there would be an increase in the melanoidin production in the malt giving it the potential for darker colour at kiln temperatures low enough to maintain diastatic power. I like the description of overheating the malt at this stage. "Will become like grease and be spoiled" This refers to when malt is stewed for a long time moisture and sugars seep out of the malt rendering it rather slick and very soft, very much like grease. By "spoiled" they could also be referring to the increase in bacteria production which would also occur under these conditions.

The 4 hour kiln time for brown malt suggests that the kiln was quite hot and/or the malt was already somewhat dry after a long germination (three weeks from start to finish in moderate weather pg 8.

Some recipes back then call for 100% brown malt so we know that it had enough diastatic power to convert itself but we also know thanks to the London and Country Brewer that brown malt had less diastatic power than pale or amber malts. When describing the kilning of brown malt the author states that it "...is often crusted and burnt, that the farinous part losses a great deal of it's essential Salts and vital Property, which frequently deceives it's ignorant brewer, that hopes to draw as much Drink from a quarter of this, as he does from pale or amber sorts" (pg.14). Another clue the author gives us regarding temperature is on the subject of frames, or the materials used for the kiln floor when he states "the Iron and Tyled one, were chiefly Invented for drying of brown Malts and saving of Fuel, for these when they come to be thorough hot will make the Corns crack and jump by the Fierceness of their Heat, so that they will be roasted or scorch'd in a little time, and after they are off the Kiln, to plump the Body of the Corn and make it take the Eye, (What I believe this means is that it will simply look better. In Wigneys 1823 Philosophical Treatise of Malting and Brewing he describes the effect of sprinkling as "giving to the malt a plump, fair appearance to the eye…") some will sprinkle Water over it that it may meet with better Market. (Malt was sold by volume) But if such malt is not used quickly, it will slacken and lose it's Spirits to a great Degree, and perhaps in half a year or less may be taken by the Whools (a small insect) and spoiled: Such hasty dryings or scorchings are also apt to bitter the Malt by burning it's skin, and therefore these Kilns are not so much used now as formerely" This is a criticism of surfaces that conduct or retain too much heat. What he is describing is "blown malt" although he does not refer to it as such. Corns that "crack and jump" and expand in size will occur when temperatures are high and the moisture inside the grain cannot escape fast enough. Blown malt was often referred to simply as brown malt after 1817 when pale malts were being used in combination with roasted malts. Blown malt was also used in combination with traditional brown malt for porters.

I am under the impression that these malts were cured hot but not as hot as one might suspect. In the Scotch Bigg Report (Thomas, Coventry and Hope 1806) a temperature of 170°F is given for brown malt which is the same curing temperature for pale malt but it is kilned while there is still moisture in the malt which will make a difference in the colour. "Malt may be made brown at a lower temperature for it is not so much the temperature, as the suddenness with which it raised, while the malt is still moist, which alters the colour." Pg. 33 However they also recorded some maltsters kilning at temperatures of 186°F and suspected some kilned as high as 212°F. This makes sense as enzymes will be destroyed rapidly over this temperature even if the malt is dry. In order to retain some enzymes but to dry the malt quickly and add colour a fire in this temperature range must have been employed. So how would these early maltsters tell if the temperature was too hot if they didn't use thermometers? Something I noticed while trying to reproduce this malt is that after I air dried the malt to around 20% moisture and started kilning, at around 225-250°F 107-121°C the malt would pop due to the rapidly escaping steam, creating blown malt. These temperatures are the upper limit for retaining enzymes so as long as there are no popping kernels your temperature will be in the safe zone and your malt will still have some diastatic power. So the two elements that are perhaps necessary for brown malt production are a warm stewing at the end of germination and curing at a temperature range of 170-212°F to create maillard reactions.

Straw, wood, fern and coal were all used to make brown malt. Straw was a prefered fuel to wood as it was cheaper and apparently had the benefit of imparting less smoke flavour to the malt, smoke flavour was considered to be an undesirable characteristic. Smoke flavour is most readily absorbed in malt when it is wet, so malt at 45% moisture absorbs more smoke flavour than malt at a low moisture content that has been allowed to wilt. Also keeping a clean burning fire will not impart that much smoke flavour.

Modern Brown Malt is kilned in a modern kiln or drum roaster at a high temperature from it's green state. There is no concern for diastatic power as this malt is always used with a base malt. This adds a roasted flavour and some bitterness.

Making Diastatic brown malt - There's not a lot of detailed information with times and temperatures before 1800 and diastatic brown malt became obsolete shortly thereafter so there is some guess work here based on my experiences trying to make this malt and other malts. Using a protein stew at 50°C or 122°F at the end of the germination like with Brumalt can give you a very dark malt. At this temperature the proteolytic and other enzymes become active and produce amino acids and simple sugars which when kilned will cause the maillard reaction. Producing a dark malt with diastatic power without this step is almost impossible, higher temperatures sacrifice enzymes. This stewing can be achieved naturally by stacking the grain towards the end of germination. These temperatures are easier to achieve with a lot of grain so if you're using small amounts at home I would recommend using a tall cooler or some kind of insulation to contain the heat produced by the respiring malt. Also the grain needs some oxygen in order to respire so do not use the cooler lid but cover with towels or something insulative that can breath. The "cheater" method would be to wait until the grain is fully modified and wilted and then transfer it to a tray, cover it with tin foil, and stew in an electric kiln before transferring it to a wood fired kiln. To mimic natural conditions I would slowly ramp up the temperature over 18-24 hours to 40-50°C and hold that temperature for 12-18 hours. This will give you a dark malt after kilning with a fair bit of acidity due to the lactic acid build up which occurs under these conditions, specifically in the 30-40°C range. Even though the description in the London and Country Brewer states to dry over a fire hot enough to dry in 4 hours, this would be after a long germination. I would dry at a low temperature until there is a 20-30% moisture content and then raise to the 170-212°F range for 4 hours.

The kiln: The tricky part in designing a kiln for brown malt is making the fire small enough and consistent enough to dry the malt without getting too hot. A small open fire would be the most basic method but requires a lot of tending and is hard to keep consistent. Two other ways that you can do this are 1. with a small rocket stove made with bricks, pictured below which would mimic a kiln but on a very small scale. Or 2. Using gassifiers using wood pellets as fuel. A gassifier is a small and very efficient stove made with cans.

It's design is pure genius as it causes the secondary gases to be burned giving you a clean fire with very little smoke. I found a can full of wood pellets usually lasts about 45 minutes and burns evenly throughout. As well, different wood pellets are available like maple, cherry and oak which can be found wherever bar-b-ques are sold. For the kiln itself, anything that's not flammable that will keep the malt about 3-4 feet above the flame will work. I've used a metal barrel (with no lid) turned upside down with a small door cut out to access the fire. I punched hundreds of holes through the top to create a heat disperser. Malt can be put directly on this surface when making a roasted or blown malt, otherwise putting the malt on a screen a few inches above this surface would be ideal. For a lid I took a hot water furnace pan and made a cut through it from the edge to the center. I then bent the pan into a cone which fit perfectly over the barrel. Insulating the lid is a good idea to prevent condensation from dripping onto your malt. I had 2- 1 gallon gassifiers and 2 small 1 quart gassifiers used in different combinations to get the temperatures where I wanted them.

Blown malt: This malt requires a hot fire usually near the end of the kilning which causes steam to "pop" the malt. The malt will sound like popcorn when it gets going. Kiln until there is 20-30% moisture. At this stage of drying the pores of the husk shrink making it harder for steam to rapidly escape without popping the husk, maltsters would also sprinkle water at this stage to "toughen the husk". (Briggs) Turn up the heat to 250- 350°F (depending on colour) to pop the kernels. Blown malt can also be made in your oven.

Blown malt on left.

Modern brown: No fire required. From the green stage kiln at 212°F 100°C for 5 hours and cure at 350°F 177°C for 40 minutes to 2 1/2 hours for a darker malt (over 100L).

Acid Malt

I use acid malt all the time to lower the pH of my mash. It doesn't take much either, maybe a few ounces and these days with brewing software it's easy to calculate how much you'll need to hit your target pH. 1% acid malt in your grain bill should lower your pH by .1. The process relies on the growth of Lactobacillus bacteria which is naturally present on the husk of the grain. It multiplies rapidly in an anaerobic environment at an optimal temperature of 37°C 99°F.

Start with some green malt after germination is complete and seal it in a ziploc bag. Try to squeeze the air out and close it so that it's airtight. The malt should still be producing Carbon dioxide so the bag may swell up after about 12 hours, just squeeze it out and make sure to seal up the bag again. Keep it at 37°C for 36 hours or more. Afterwards take it out and spread it on a screen at the same temperature for as long as it takes to dry. Do not cure this malt. Results may vary depending on the growth of bacteria. Do not use more than 10% in your beer.

Wheat

Wheat malts are made in a similar way to barley, with the main difference being the lack of a husk. This lack of fibre necessitates the use of rice hulls when brewing with larger amounts of wheat malt to prevent a stuck sparge. Use 10% by weight of rice hulls in your recipe. As well, without a protective husk the acrospires are exposed and unprotected so care must be taken when turning the germinating grain. If the acrospire breaks off, the grain dies. To avoid this turn grains by pouring them from one container to another. Steeping is also more rapid, without the husk the grain absorbs water faster.

Steep grain to 45% moisture content at 10-15°C 50-59°F. It usually takes only 2 - 8 hour steeps with an 8 hour air rest. Germinate at 12-15°C 54-59°F for a minimum of 5 days or until modified.
For a pale wheat malt kiln at 45°C 113°F (Air-on temperature) until moisture is below 10%.
Cure between 170-190°F 77-88°C depending on colour desired for 3-5 hours
To make caramel, roasted or munich type wheat malts follow the directions for barley.

O

The reason why you don't see a lot of 100% oat malt beer is because malted oats do not taste very good. The flavour and aroma is very similar to green corn husks freshly shucked off the cob. It's not a corn flavour but a grassy green flavour. I have not experienced this flavour in unmalted oats. I first assumed that the flavour was coming from the oat husks but this is not the case as I've also malted hulled oats to see if there was a difference and there was not. It's a hard flavour to get used to and can be mistaken as a mustiness in the beer, so oats are not a grain I'd recommend malting. Toast them or use them raw instead. If you're curious or if that's the only grain you have access to or if you really like the taste of grass and corn husks then here are some tips to malting oats:

Oats will absorb water faster than barley as their husk is looser, hulled oats absorb even faster. For oats with the husk, one steep of 11-12 hours will probably give you enough moisture to reach 40% For hulled oats, one 8 hour steep should be enough.
For some reason, I have achieved better germination rates using lower moisture contents   (38-40%) this may be something you want to experiment with further.
Germinate at 16-18°C 61-64°F for 5-7 days
Kiln as you would for barley malts.

Spelt and Emmer

Malt these ancient grains just like modern wheat, although I find that Emmer being the smaller of the two germinates a day or two faster and may take a little less time to dry. Shoot for a 42-45% moisture content. Steep between 10-13°C 50-55°F and germinate at 13-15°C 55-59°F. Turn every 8 hours or so depending on temperature but handle carefully.

Because they dry fast without a husk it's possible to dry them at room temperature. Spread out to about an inch in depth on a screen. Aim a fan that's a foot or two away directly at the malt. It should be below 10% moisture in about 24 hours. Stir occasionally. Once it's below 10% cure in your oven at 185°F 85°C for 5 hours or whatever curing schedule you've chosen. Shake the roots off with a strainer and it's good to go. Like wheat, when mashing include 10% rice hulls, by weight to avoid a stuck sparge. For example if I was using 10lbs. of Spelt or Emmer I would include 1 pound of rice hulls mixed into the mash.

Bibliography

Baverstock, James, J. H. Baverstock. (1824). *Treatises on Brewing*. London: Printed for G. & W.B. Whittaker

Briggs, D. E. *Malts and Malting*. (1998). 1st ed. London: Blackie Academic and Professional.

Briggs, D.E, J.S. Hough, R. Stevens. (1971). *Malting and Brewing Science*.
London: Chapman & Hall.

Briggs, D.E. "Accelerated Malting: A Review of Some Lessons of the Past from the United Kingdom" American Society of Brewing Chemists 1987.

Calpas, J., Howard, R., Turkinton, K., Clear, R., Evans, I. "Fusarium Head Blight of Barley and Wheat" Agdex 110/632-1. (2003). Alberta Ministry of Agriculture and Forestry. Web. 25 Nov. 2017.

Clark, Christine. (1978). *The British Malting Industry Since 1830*. London, U.K. Hambledon Press.

Clerk, Jean de. (1957). *A Textbook of Brewing Vol. 1*. London: Chapman & Hall.

Clerk, Jean de. (1958). *A Textbook of Brewing Vol. 2*. London: Chapman & Hall

Ellis, William. (1737). *The London and Country Brewer*. The 3rd ed. London: Printed for J. and J. Fox.

Ford, William. (1862). *A Practical Treatise on Malting and Brewing*.

London, U.K. Published by the Author.

"Fusarium Head Blight of Barley and Wheat" Agdex 110/632-1. (2003) Alberta Ministry of Agriculture and Forestry. Web. 12 Feb. 2015.

Kunze, Wolfgang, Susan Pratt. (2004). *Technology: Brewing and Malting.* 3rd ed.
    Berlin: VLB.

Kunze, Wolfgang, *Technology: Brewing & Malting* 5th English Edition Berlin: VLB. 2014, p 180.

Lancaster, Hugh. (1908). Reprinted 2014. Hayward, CA: White Mule Press.

Lévy, Lucien. La practique du maltage: leçons professées en 1897-1898 a l'Institut des fermentations de l'Université nouvelle de Bruxelles. Charleston, SC: Bibliolife, 2017

Loftus, W.R. (1876). The Maltster: *A Compendious Treatise on the Art of Malting in All Its   Branches.* London: W.R. Loftus.

"Managing Diseases" Alberta Barley Organization. N.p., n.d. Web. 30 Nov. 2017.

McLelland, M., Panchuk, K., Green, B., Campbell, D., Dr. Harvey, B., Dr. Rossnagel, B., Foster, J., Dr. Kendall, N. "Malting Barley" Agdex 114/20-2 Revised 2009. Alberta Ministry of Agriculture and Forestry. Web. Nov. 30 1017.

Muller, C., Methner, FJ. "An accelerated malting procedure-influences on malt quality and cost savings by reduced energy consumption and malting losses" J.Inst. Brew. 2015, 121:181-192.

Narziss, L. and Back, W. (2012). Die Bierbrauerei. Wiley-Vch.

Neate, S., McMullen, M. *Barley Disease Handbook.* North Dakota State University, (2005). Web 30 Nov. 2017.

"Official Grain Grading Guide" *Canadian Grain Commision.* Government of Canada. 6-3 - 6-26 (2017). Web. 30 Nov. 2017.

Petit, P. (1904). *Brasserie and Malterie.* Paris: Gauthier-Villars.

Stopes, Henry. (1885). *Malt and Malting: An Historical, Scientific and Practical Treatise.*
    London: F.W. Lyon.

Thomson, T., Hope, Coventry. (1806). *Report of the Experiments Made by the Direction of the Honourable Board of Excise In Scotland, to Ascertain the relative Qualities of Malt made from Barley and Scotch Bigg.* Selection of Reports and Papers of the House of Commons. Vol. 15. Malting Brewing and Distillation. 1836.

Thomson, T., Stewart, W. (1849). *Brewing and Distillation.* Edinburgh: Adam and Charles Black.

Tizard, W. L. (1846). *The Theory and Practice of Brewing.* London: Published by Author.

Wahl, R., Henius, M. (1908). *American Handy Book of the Brewing, Malting and Auxiliary Trades, Volume Two.* Chicago: Wahl-Henius Institute.

Wigney, George Adolphus. (1823). *A Philosophical Treatise on Malting and Brewing.*
    Brighton, England: Worthington Press.

Dr. Wright, B. "Molds, Mycotoxins and Their Effects On Horses" (2003) *Ontario Ministry of Food, Agriculture and Rural Affairs* Web. 12 Feb. 2015.

87543955R00054

Made in the USA
Columbia, SC
15 January 2018